T0195750

DISCOVER YOUR GOAL

Zdeňka Jordánová

Order this book online at www.trafford.com
or email orders@trafford.com

Most Trafford titles are also available at major online book retailers.

Printed in the United States of America.

ISBN: 978-1-4907-3373-9 (sc)
ISBN: 978-1-4907-3374-6 (hc)
ISBN: 978-1-4907-3375-3 (e)

Library of Congress Control Number: 2014906948

2nd English edition
1st English edition, 2011, 3rd Czech edition, 2013 published by
Vodnář Publishers, http://www.volny.cz/naklvodnar

Trafford rev. 06/05/2014

www.trafford.com
North America & international
toll-free: 1 888 232 4444 (USA & Canada)
fax: 812 355 4082

Contents

Acknowledgments

I dedicate this book to all those who supported my—in the beginning, diffident—intention to start writing and patiently brought to me further messages that led my steps. Thanks to all who sincerely asked the question "Where can we read all that?" at my lectures. Thank you to all my clients, students, and friends for their wonderful stories, which were a great source of guidance, and thanks for the trust with which they imparted the stories to me. Thanks to my partner, Peter, who always believed that I have enough theme to write about; thanks to my friend Alena, who always waited for the next chapter to read; and above all, thanks to my three children, Michala, Matous, and Samuel, who always showed me the way and supported me in my decisions.

Thank you.

Introduction

Hello, hello, it's planet Earth calling!
*Hello, hello, it's us, **people,***
the inhabitants of the Earth!
We can do practically anything,
but after centuries, we are still
looking for just one thing:
happiness . . .

We've tried everything, but for some reason, whatever we try ends up not working. We have grand plans and think that once we've achieved them, they'll bring us happiness . . . Or that once we find him or her, we'll be happy. Most of the time, once we get what we want, we find out that we still have to do this and that to be happy—maybe even that stuff too. We're constantly searching for what needs to be done so that *It* will finally arrive.

We're constantly searching for that particular world, that particular person, and that particular everything for it, simply put, to work. We're all always waiting for something, for something amazing, which we expect will arrive at any moment. We all know that it definitely exists. Even those who are saying that they've stopped believing know somewhere deep in their hearts that something that makes sense must exist . . .

Human beings are the only living things on planet Earth who have the ability to materialize their ideas. That's just the way things

1

work, whether we are aware of it or not. That means that if our intentions are set up so that we're "searching" for happiness, then our mind materializes "searching." We'll probably keep searching until we change our intention. So stop searching and start **creating** what you're searching for. It'll be a little bit more fun, because when you are able to do something yourself, it always makes you feel good. At least that's true for the persons who are willing to take their life into their own hands and try something, for the persons who are tired of this endless searching and senseless waiting.

> **Stop searching and start creating what you're searching for.**

Another difficulty encountered during the quest for happiness is searching at the wrong time. Most of us are living the future and are waiting for when it will finally "happen." Others of us are living the past, where it already "happened," and there's no chance of changing it because it's already a long time gone. We forget that there's only one right time to do something—the present. Some people's lives look like this: they are looking forward to retirement, when they'll finally have time for their hobbies, when they won't have to do anything and they'll be "free." Dear friends, have you ever seen an old lion who's spent his entire life in a cage? In the twilight of his life, the zookeepers open his cage and say, "Our apologies, dear lion, you can go now. You're free!" You can guess what happens next. So don't put anything off because . . .

> **The only time for creating is now—in the present.**

Another important implication of this is that we have to delimit the space we're searching in, at least a little bit. Most of us choose the outside world—in other words, the world around us. However, that world is huge from the perspective of one person who's searching for something—it's infinite—and so it's no surprise that we sometimes lose hope when we're unable to find what we're searching for a long time. If we would admit that we are actually really searching inside ourselves, we might be a little happier: The space inside us is not quite as large . . .

Everything we are looking for in the outside world we already have inside ourselves. Happiness is within us!

I once read a story about a being named Mary, who decided to go to Earth because she had heard that all over the planet, they play a strange game. It's a very popular and widespread game. It is called the Problem Game. Mary enjoyed playing popular games, so she really wanted to learn how to play, and to play it. However, it wasn't that easy for her because she was a universal being, and so she naturally worked in line with universal laws; she was in perfect union with herself, with others, and with the rest of the universe. In other words, she just wasn't capable of creating any messes in her life. She resolved all her problems immediately—because nothing was ever actually really a problem. She just couldn't understand how to play the game . . .

We have learned to "play" this game perfectly! Our countless problems come in such superb variety. We play so wonderfully that we've substituted the problem game for life, and we act as if all this is completely normal . . . The biggest problem is that we are always saying that we "couldn't do it." We're masters at creating endless rationalizations and objective truths. But if we were able to expend this massive amount of energy, which we are using to create excuses and creating other false rules about why certain things cannot be achieved, then we probably would have managed to do everything a long time ago. We've bought into various "wise" assertions, like "Few people are lucky enough to do what they enjoy," "You can't get what you really want from life," "Responsibilities come first, fun second," or "I'm never going to have any money." We often hear "You know, you'll never find someone who suits you" or "Relationships are all about making constant compromises." Or on the other hand, "Relationships are a battle," "You know, after you turn fifty, there's nothing to look forward to, just pain and illness," "Your kids are just headaches . . ." or "You can't get anything in life by playing by the rules . . ." We've embraced illness, allergies, and pain as part of life, which we strengthen ever more either by ignoring it all or by taking different kinds of pills, which usually don't solve the problems anyway. If the cause isn't cured, the symptoms usually continue elsewhere. We've accepted alcohol as part of life, thanks to which we may completely miss out on our lives. We've accepted smoking as part of life, contaminating the planet and wasting infinitely beautiful moments, all because we've lost the ability to live in the present. We've accepted narcotics as a way of escaping life. We've accepted drugs as a form of self-destruction and as a way of avoiding our responsibility for anything. Pain, pain in endless manifestations . . . On top of all that, instead of dealing with our own lives, we watch the stories of people we don't even know on TV. We vicariously live out their lives instead of our own. We spend our time giving our energy to other people for them to reach their goals—like when we watch sports on TV, during which we ourselves remain disconnected from life and don't give our bodies any movement. Why do we do all this? What sort of advantages does it give us?

At first glance, it may seem we get none. But don't be mistaken. No one does anything unless it brings them at least some seeming advantages. Maybe this is upsetting you . . . Imagine a woman who can't walk. Perhaps she would protest, saying, "What sort of advantages do I get out of not being able to walk? Well, please be so kind as to fill me in!"

"Well, perhaps it's in the fact that you don't have to walk anywhere and that your children take care of you. They bring the shopping home every day, and you get to see them every day."

"Yeah, so what?" she fumes. After chatting for a while, perhaps she would tell me that if she weren't sick, then her kids would never visit her. And so we have a story. So . . .

Nobody does anything that he or she doesn't want to!
Except . . .

Each of us is a perfect being who desires to express themselves to his or her full potential. Every one of us has his or her perfect and individual goal, which he or she has decided to fulfill on earth. We chose the precisely appropriate conditions for our birth, the appropriate parents, and the most appropriate location. We have the ability to materialize our intentions, because everything the human race has created began as just ideas.

Our life is the sum of all our conscious and subconscious intentions . . .

and if we track what's "happening" in our lives, we can learn a lot about ourselves. Especially once we understand that nothing just happens—but that we do it ourselves—we gain great opportunities to create, and the adventure begins. The more we are aware of our creation, the more we will be thrilled by life and our endless potential.

That's why you should remember your childhood dreams and look for connections with your life, do things that attract you, and create situations in which you feel good. Don't let yourself get discouraged, and keep on going. Do what you enjoy. If you're not sure what that is, keep trying until you find it. You will be happy on the way. Don't try to be perfect because you're already perfect. You just need to keep moving on because there's always something to improve. You can achieve everything you desire as long as you truly believe that you can achieve it.

We create life through our everyday choices, so let's take responsibility for what we have created. If we don't like it, we can change it!

A little girl once came up to me and said, "Zdeňka, I'd like to fly." "So go ahead and fly!" I said. "And what if I fall?" the girl asked. "If you believe that you won't fall, you won't," I responded. She thought about it deeply for a while and then inquired, "What if I believe and I still fall?" I explained that that was impossible because if she were to fall, that would mean she didn't truly believe. She thought about it once more and asked seriously, "And when will I know that I truly believe?" I smiled and waited. "Aha!" She suddenly understood. "Once I don't fall, right?"

It's true that you don't necessarily need to begin with flying, but stop playing that old, worn-out Problem Game. Take responsibility for your life and start creating what you want because it's time to move on . . .

Chapter 1

The Connections between Us—
We Want to Be "At One"

How many of you have the feeling that the problem you have isn't so huge and unbeatable after all—when you find out that someone else has the same, or almost the same, problem as you do? Imagine that you wake up in the morning with a yucky feeling that you don't have such a nice day ahead of you (you yourself are responsible for its organization and your attitude to it, of course), and your head begins to hurt. You don't feel well, and you are concentrated on that problem. That means that you are giving it all your energy. It sounds strange, but maybe the outcome of this is that when you step onto the bus, you meet an acquaintance who at once begins to complain that her head hurts. By chance. We are like magnets, and we pull into our lives situations that we need to understand. You are suspicious about it, but it seems that all at once you feel a little bit better. You continue, reaching work, where you find out that the secretary has a headache today too. You feel really weird about this, but every time you hear this, you feel a particular sense of relief. And maybe, well, your head has kind of stopped hurting. You have the feeling that your problem has been solved. Three people in your surroundings have the same problems, then. Maybe you say to yourself that it probably doesn't have anything to do with you; it probably has something to do with "some sunspots" or something like that . . .

And you don't have to do anything about that; you don't have to come to realize anything. It doesn't even occur to you that the fact that your head is hurting is your inner state. "If there are more of us," you say, "then it is definitely being caused by something outside of me, and I most likely don't have anything to do with it." And so we suffer collectively, and what's more, we think that it's normal.

This is the alcoholism of our planet. We are all mutually intertwined, and we want to be "at one." The result of these efforts is that we aren't able to be ourselves. Most of us even think that it's impossible. Most of us suffer from sameness, which gives us a fictitious feeling of safety and confirms the rightness of our behavior. Those of us who are braver reject this sameness—and often we think that that means that we have to be mean and severe to other people so that we can be ourselves and so that they leave us alone. Most of us feel like we are pulled into other people's problems and that at the same time we pull other people into our own problems, and we don't feel it. Later we can't tell anymore which problems are ours and which are other people's problems. When it has got to this point, then neither we nor they can solve the problems. I imagine it like this:

Joe is going for a beer. He knows that there will be problems and that he will get drunk again, but "it is stronger than he is." He meets a friend by chance on the way who has decided that he's not going to go to the pub anymore because he wants to start a new life. Joe tests him. "O'Hara, man, come with me just for the one! Don't make like you don't belong anymore, or that you don't like beer anymore. Come on, old pal, we'll bullshit a little, you'll relax a little, you're all stressed out."

"No, I really don't drink anymore," says a slightly unsure O'Hara. And now Joe gets angry. "So now you're so stuck up that you'll let your old friend drink by himself and wreck his health? You're a great friend . . ." O'Hara is on the fence, a feeling of guilt eroding his resolution, which he slowly puts aside for another time. "Well, really, if it is a question of your health, then I guess I will go . . . Hey, man, I didn't mean for it to come out like that . . ." And so his resolutions are gone, in the service of higher ideals—in this case, the ideal of "friendship," and in the interest of "everyone's good health."

We (each of us) are the source of our own problems!
We are also the source of our own solutions!

Each of us is unique, and we are going down the path of our own experiences. What is good for one person doesn't have to be good for another. We are all on the path to freedom! On the path to freely expressing one's self in this world! Some of us, for example, need to learn to follow the rules on our path to be at ease, because they are all the time going against something and fighting. Others need to break the rules sometimes in order to learn to take responsibility for their decisions even in situations when someone else doesn't like it. We are all actually learning to take responsibility for our lives.

The situations that we create in life are lessons—they are there for us to understand something. If a situation happens more than once in our lives and we don't like it, then we need to look for a model of our dysfunctional thinking and behavior. We are not always consciously conscious of the way in which we bring about the formation of a certain reality in our lives. What we know and say on the conscious level is only about 20 percent of everything we do and notice. The rest of it functions somehow "differently." One example of this is our subconsciousness, where, on the basis of stored situations and lived-through experiences from childhood and on the basis of our parents' and teachers' assessments, we brought into our lives specific attitudes and opinions about ourselves, about life, and the people around us. These systems of belief don't always serve us well. Consciously, we are not aware of following these systems, but these systems are directing us.

Imagine, for example, that you have been planning for a long time to buy a house. Your intention, however, keeps on not being realized. Either you don't have the money or it isn't the right house or it isn't the right time—how many times we make excuses when something isn't working out. Somewhere inside ourselves, we of course have all the information we need to discover where the problem is. Sometimes you just have to listen to what you yourself are saying. Perhaps you are telling your friends about how your parents never wanted a house. Maybe you are explaining to your friends that they didn't really want to work themselves down to the bone, so they just lived in an apartment. So if we ask, we get an answer. Why don't you have your own house yet? There are some "truths" we just keep repeating without being conscious of their contents. Listen, and you will hear the answer: "I don't want a house because I don't want to work myself to death." What is it really? What is my real intention? Whoever seeks finds, even though it won't always be this simple, of course. So now all that is left to do is to change that subconscious intention to a conscious one and to understand that I can have a house and I don't have to work myself down to the bone. For sometimes we take even nonsensical life laws into our rules, and by the fact that these nonsensical life laws are endlessly repeated in our external world, we come to "believe" in them. In this case, the law of preserving life is the paramount one for our life now, and unless we change that law, we won't have the house. In reality, we are the ones who refused to buy the house. What should we do? Change our attitude and make a new, conscious, intention. And one more small thing—believe in it . . . and act to that effect. How will we know that we have understood and changed everything? Well, that's when we have a house and we don't slave over it!

Free yourself from the limits that are holding you back from expressing yourself.

The highest good for you is also the highest good for others . . .

even though it doesn't always look that way (at least according to other people's reactions).

One of these significant limits is that we have learned to give other people precedence over ourselves. So we often think that other people know better than we do what is good for us. "I know what is good for you, I am experienced," say our parents, and they know "better" than us which school is good for us, which friends, which partners, and so on. And we listen to them because at the beginning, when we were small, that was the only way—and later we learn to take advantage of certain benefits we get from it, when we don't have to take responsibility for our lives. That way, we always find someone else who is responsible for what doesn't suit us.

I found the passage in Marlo Morgan's book *Mutant Message Down Under* fascinating, where the author describes how, in the framework of the community of Unity, Australian aborigines don't give their children names. Each child creates his or her own name. The aborigines assume that each person has his or her own goal and work to do and that sooner or later, this will be expressed. They observe little children and wait for what they do, what they find interesting and fun. When children reveal themselves, they support children in their activities because they believe that the children know best who they are. If, for instance, a boy starts to hunt or get food, they call him Little Hunter. Little Hunter decides for himself when he is ready to become Big Hunter, and everyone celebrates his success with him. The goal of the individual becomes the goal of the society, because we are all connected. From this point of view, it is obvious that the competing and the comparisons, which we so value in our world, are nonsense.

We are all unique.

Therefore, we will be in unity with the whole only when we are in unity with ourselves. The whole—our society, nation, country, planet, universe, everything—will be more perfect and happier if we are ourselves, because this is useful for everyone. To be part of the whole doesn't mean to be the same as everyone else, to have the same worries and problems, but it means that being different, we are looking for a new shape of the world in our own image. And then we will truly be a part of the whole; we will stand in our uniqueness in **unity** with all others.

Chapter 2

_(3) (2)_

Coincidences Don't Happen by Chance

Let me tell you a story.

Once I had an appointment for a checkup with my dentist. After I was shown into her office . . . Just so you understand, my dentist is a serious lady and an excellent doctor. She has a little bit of a tendency to continually complain about the world around her and really doesn't like to hear that the way she is doing things could have anything to do with what "happens" to her—as she likes to name it. She is very skeptical in regard to making changes in her life. She's a firm believer in "medications." By medications we mean all that solves our problem without our endeavor and understanding. The dentist knows what I do for a living, and I think that it interests her very much, but she has a problem accepting the simplicity of certain things. Most of all, I think that she simply "likes" her problems, and after all, medications are medications. So . . .

I stepped into her office, and my dear dentist was lying on her delightful dentist's chair. She had a wet towel on her forehead and said, "Ms. Jordánová, I think I'll finally let you unblock me." What an honor, I said to myself and waited to see what happens next because the tone of her voice was rather curious and was resonating with an unusual color. Do you know that feeling when you're experiencing something extraordinary and a unique feeling of oneness and matter-of-factness sweeps over you in spite of the fact that everything seems so completely unbelievable at the same time? "Picture this," she continued. "I had a new patient. She was here for the first time. I hadn't met her before. Before she came in, while treating a man, I cut this finger." She emphatically displayed her left index finger, which was wrapped in bandage. I waited, full of suspense, for her to continue because I could sense the wonder of the moment. She breathed in and continued, "I got angry with myself because it's difficult working with a bandage on." In line with her usual custom, she blamed her "awkward finger," which had become the current source of her problems. She continued, "Imagine that the new patient comes in and I start telling her about what happened to me and I jokingly offer her my injured finger 'For sale' and I present her with the bandaged culprit. You wouldn't believe it, Ms. Jordánová, but she looked up at me and put her left hand in front of my eyes and said, 'Sold.' Her left index finger was missing."

So, my dear friends, there's no such thing as a coincidence, because everything is simply a reaction to our own actions, and the Universe is very creative in the ways it informs us of what we have done. If we're not willing to perceive our actions, then we have the feeling that things are just "happening" or arriving or coming together by chance, etc. If my dear dentist willingly offers her own finger (which she herself injured) as a problem, then this action, interpreted by universal laws, causes a reaction. Consequently, she gets the opportunity to see what it would be like being a member of a group of people who don't have fingers. The choice is up to you!

Sometimes we are able to perceive so-called accidents as the warning signs that they truly are. They allow us to look into the reality we are now in the process of creating. But even seeing these signs doesn't help most people gain understanding. One Arabian proverb says that if we make a mistake once, it doesn't mean that we'll necessarily make it again; but if we make the same mistake a second time, we're sure to make it a third time because it has already become entrenched in us. However, not all of us are willing to learn from our experiences and not all of us are willing to contemplate upon a specific situation that has repeated itself a number of times in life. Take tripping over the same doorstep for the third time. Some people may ultimately decide to lift their foot, but others will prefer to remove the doorstep. Then maybe they would start tripping over another doorstep—the option of lifting their foot finally hits them once they realize that the next doorstep couldn't be removed. It could go either way (or even another way altogether), but in both cases, it's important to perceive all the messages around us and integrate them into our lives because all of them are messages about us, for us.

Everything is symbols that we can read from if we are attuned and are paying attention. We can read about our lives. The city and street we live in and what kind of neighbors we have aren't coincidences. We choose everything either through our own decisions or through the stances we take in regard to the experiences we've lived through. I really enjoy paying close attention to the names not only of people but also of animals and to the acronyms of companies. I'm not quite sure if I'd entrust my money to a financial agent whose name is Mr. Poor, nor if I'd want to live in a village called Dunghill, which I once saw in a banner at the edge of the village, encouraging locals to participate in a local beautification activity: "Make Dunghill more beautiful!"[1] My own name is a source of much inspiration because my maiden name was Moses, and my husband's name, Jordan, naturally fascinated me as well, along with a host of other things, of course, about him. Our children are called Michala, Matous, and Samuel. I don't know, but they just couldn't have been named differently. What about the young lady who always had problems with her voice, who later married a man named Mr. Whimper and became Mrs. Whimper? What about Mrs. Wheat, whose maiden name was Farmer? She inherited some fields in Slavetown and didn't want to work like a slave on them anymore but instead to happily make a good, honest living out of them. And how about the environmentalist specializing in rare birds Mr. Sparrow? What are the private gardening services of Mr. Nettle like? And

---

[1] Czech family and place-names tend to seem ridiculous to English speakers. Other examples of common surnames are Doesn't-eat-bread and Jumpedout.

what about Mr. Twig, the director of the botanical garden, and his beautiful lectures? When our house started becoming too damp, we called upon the services of a dampproofing firm. Upon meeting the firm's representative, Mr. Littlewater, we tried to explain that there's probably more than a little water under our house. There are many other fantastic examples that are worth thinking about. It's worth your while to find the origin and translations of your names because—and I'm convinced of this—they contain hints about your goal and the life tasks you need to accomplish. On some level, they can clue us in. So . . .

Notice everything around you because nothing is a coincidence—it is all simply reactions to our conscious and subconscious actions. All these are lessons and messages for us.

Be attentive to life around you and notice how, in connection to what is happening, you feel. The feelings you receive from your body give precise information about your situation, but you have to be aware of them and understand them. Always take note of what doesn't seem to "fit in" in a given situation or what otherwise seems strange. All the significant messages in your life are "unusual" in some way. For example, if you happen to cause yourself pain, that means that you've definitely wasted a great deal of useful information on how to do things differently and you've wasted the opportunity to avoid possible pain and suffering.

A few years ago, I had a car accident. I wrecked my car and broke some bones. This was what happened: It was during the beginning stages of my work. I was working with lots of people, and I was enthusiastic about the great changes in my life. People around me were feeling better, and I was astounded by how wonderfully it was all working. One day, my phone rang. A man asked me if I'd be able to advise him, long distance, on how to find something he had lost. "We'll figure something out," I said. "What did you lose?"

"Sunglasses," the man said. "And they were practically antiques. I never wore them. I had them on a little shelf behind a pane of glass, and I used to look at them all the time. They were always in the same spot, and then all of a sudden, they were gone. I'd really like them back . . ." *A weirdo,* I said to myself and gave him an appointment for the following week. It all seemed very strange to me; I just couldn't get my head around it. One morning three days later, I was driving in my car, heading east. The sun was shining beautifully, and then all at once, the horizon was flooded with gorgeous light and I wasn't able to see the road. Everything was shining and then . . . crash . . . and all those broken bones. I didn't have any sunglasses.

Everything is a symbol. Learn to understand.

Chapter 3

DISEASE = DIS EASE[2]
Ill at Ease because You Don't
Have Power Over Your Life

When we are sick, we don't have power over our lives and, therefore, cannot make free decisions. How often do we hear around us "I would like to vacuum, but my back really hurts," "I would exercise, but with my back, I can barely move," "I would love to ride a bike, but my knees are all screwed up," "I want to sing, but I get so hoarse that I don't even try," "I would take a vacation, but I can't," or "With my gallbladder?" "With my stomach?" "With my . . ." and so on. Sometimes I have the feeling that some people are actually proud of all the things they can't do. If conversation comes around to one of their problems, they begin to report all their ailments, illustrating all the aspects of their sickness: when it began, whose fault it was, and mainly everything that they could no longer do and why, or perhaps how much it bothers them. But "what can you do about it, you have to hang in there".

---

[2]   The wordplay (and etymology) in Czech is different, and the author uses the comparison throughout the chapter. "Nemoc" in Czech means sickness, and "ne moc" means (1) not to have power or strength or, simply, (2) not to have much.

Sickness is another very ingenious way not to go after our goal, a reason not to reach our dream because, simply, we can't. It fascinates me that people really believe that they can't do certain things because certain parts of their body necessary for the activity don't work, and it never occurs to them that perhaps they are creating the problem themselves precisely because they don't want to have to do the aforementioned activity. We pretend as if sickness was sent to us by "something"—something that doesn't have anything to do with us, something that has power over us—and we get very upset when someone doesn't take it seriously.

You could even say that health problems are socially acceptable universal excuses for any kind of incompetence or possible failure. "I couldn't run because I had pain in my knees," and everyone understands this because, after all, everyone has had pain in their knees. But what if he had a pain in his knee in order that he didn't have to run? Nonsense, you say? "Why would he do that?" you say. Well, it occurs to me . . . maybe he knew that he couldn't come in first.

Let's look at it like this: Our body is a perfect symbol. Our body is perfect and wonderful, and it helps us live our lives in a physical reality because it is giving us perfect information all the time about ourselves. Our thoughts are materialized through our body, and it is through our feelings that we get perfect feedback about every step we take. If we weren't always suppressing our emotions and were able to express them anytime (what a mess that would be, you might say), we would most likely never be sick. In our entrenched reality, we aren't able to do it . . . Let me tell you a story.

Once upon a time, there was a little boy who wanted so very much to play with his colored blocks with his mother. He wanted to build a chimney. He was one year old; he wasn't able to speak yet, so he stood next to his mother and pulled on her skirt while his mother stood at the cooking range, stirring the soup. She had read in a parenting book that babies were supposed to eat at this time of day, and so that was what she was going to do. Moms have a tendency to believe other people about how they should deal with their children, because they have forgotten that they themselves know best. Their children get very frustrated with this—they want tuned-in moms they can talk to and communicate with. So our little boy continued with his request, but mom knows what she knows. "I'll just make you a nice soup, just for you. Come on, give me a break, I am doing this for you . . ." And of course, the little boy didn't understand that at all. It's not what he wanted. The little boy didn't understand what's going on—why his mother could not, because of his needs, do something that he himself really wanted. (This is our first lesson in manipulation and emotional blackmail—when our parents do something that we don't want at all and maintain that they are doing it for us.) The little boy didn't know how to deal with this. He was disappointed and felt not listened to and rejected. This feeling led him away from being tuned in and experiencing the present moment, and because he felt bad, he forgot that he was standing under the table. He stood up and banged and got a bump on the head. "Ow, that hurts," he said, and he began to cry. Pay attention because now something really interesting happened: Mom threw down her spoon and ran to her little boy. "Don't cry, pumpkin, it's okay. Mommy will blow on it. Give me those little fingers . . . see. Okay, so let's build a chimney. A chimney. Chimney." Quick as lightning, mom built a chimney, and the little boy marveled. "So there it is," he marveled, "that's very interesting." He shook his head. "A little while ago, it didn't work, and now it's working. What changed? Aha, the pain . . . and now I've got it—if I am in pain, I get what I want." From that time on, it stayed with the boy that he has a guaranteed method to get what he wants, a method certified for endless uses, which works perfectly.

And because it works, we begin to use it. Each of us has our own story about how we gathered these experiences. Some of us don't even bother to make the effort to say anything anymore because we know that "we won't get anything anyway," and so it's better to use the guaranteed method right from the start. Some of us don't believe that we will get any attention any other way or for any other reason than for the fact that we have pain. And so we suffocate or cover our body in itching eczema or we have angina or various other chronic illnesses, and THEY try and try . . . and they are full of fear, and we have the impression that our illness pays off.

We give up our control over ourselves, and we are controlled by the fact that we control others. We don't get tired by these feelings of new power, which we wouldn't need, of course, if we believed that we can have what we want in our lives.

Once I worked with a woman who had cancer. Her condition was very serious, and doctors gave her very little chance of recovery. She was in great pain, and she wanted to try something else besides the doctors. If, in our lives, we want to get rid of a problem, it is important to understand why we are creating it ourselves, because

no one does anything that he or she doesn't want to do.

This is true even, paradoxically, when we are harming ourselves—it is important to figure out what we are getting out of it and whether we are in fact getting something out of it or whether we only think that. Cancer is suppressed anger, which, when we don't express it, we turn it against ourselves. In other words, we don't take care of and don't stand up for ourselves. There was a wonderful woman who had decided at the last minute to understand her sickness. She realized that now, everything in her life was perfect, "heavenly" even. Her husband, with whom she had three children, had all throughout their married life come home late, hung out at bars, and run around with other women. Now he came home right after work, did the shopping, took care of the children, and even looked after her. He felt guilty about his past behavior, and his sick wife "knew" that if she were to get well, that he would return to his old routine. She wasn't willing to risk losing her "advantageous" position and decided to sacrifice her life for this illusion. She told me herself of her decision and that the time she spent in her husband's attention and care was worth it. I always remember this woman with love and am grateful to her for the story she gave me. She passed away—and that is also a choice that must be respected.

The more we give up our own power and the more our problems materialize in our body, the way back becomes harder and harder. After a certain age, some of us are convinced that if they woke up one morning and nothing was hurting, then they must be dead—everyone according to their beliefs. What we think, we become.

Our body is a perfect symbol of our thinking. Our illnesses are symbolic. They are messages about us, for us, and if we understand them and change our behaviors, we don't have to be ill anymore.

It is up to us to learn to use these messages. Our body is perfect, and it works in an endlessly creative and patient way. What are we constantly doing to this body? How are we treating this perfect instrument for self-knowledge? How are we taking care of our splendorous and singular body? How do we nourish ourselves? How many things do we pass off as food when they really have nothing to do with food? We drink alcohol and smoke, we live unhealthily and don't move very much, we gain weight, and we don't love ourselves. Other people's bodies seem to us to be better, more attractive, and more beautiful. We are constantly dissatisfied, and we don't do anything about it. When someone points this out to us, some of us say, "Well, you know, I have to die of something." We are getting over our illnesses without ever resting, and we don't pay them any attention. We often treat our cars more reverently than our bodies. Think about it like this: Your car runs out of oil. The oil light is shining, and anyone who is interested in using their car in the future heads toward the nearest gas station to put more oil in. But you will always find someone clever, who thinks he can outwit the machine— he won't put any more oil in. What's more, he removes the blinking oil light and drives on. "I don't see anything, nothing's blinking." You probably think that he's crazy and won't get very far that way. But this is the same thing we are doing with our bodies when, instead of understanding the meaning of our sicknesses, we go to the pharmacy and gobble up something expensive. Our body isn't always willing to give up on its warning signal and often tries other much more urgent ways to give us information about our attitude. We try to be clever about it. We go to the doctor; we believe that they know better than ourselves what is wrong with our bodies. And of course, the doctor knows. "If the medicine doesn't help, then we will just take it out" and so on. "The organ that is bothering you has to come out, it's gone haywire." And our desperate and unheard body looks for another warning indicator.

Currently there are many good books out about the meanings of our illnesses. I believe that this information should be included in school curricula, because so many people have no idea that they are causing their sicknesses themselves—even in the case of proven infections, when only our system of belief decides whether we catch that one or not.

I always remember my youngest son's first-grade teacher, Magda, with great regard. We were acquaintances, and she was aware of my interests. She never called in question my son Sam's reasoning. Sam, since childhood, had heard stories from my consultations, and he understood the connections between his life's creations and his responsibility for them. Once, Sam's teacher told me about a time when the class was on their way back from their weekly swimming lesson. Magda came out from the swimming pavilion with the children whose hot bodies were steaming in the cool air. She instructed them to put on their hats so they wouldn't catch a cold. My son Sam got angry when he heard that and said defiantly, "Mrs. Teacher, that isn't in my plan," and didn't put his hat on. The teacher took a beat and reacted in a wonderful way, saying, "All right, everyone, hats on. But Sam doesn't have to since it's not in his plan." Sam didn't get sick because it really wasn't in his plan.

But my children didn't always behave in such a mature manner even though they know all about the relationship between their thoughts and the reactions of their bodies. One morning before school, my daughter, Michala, explained to me that her throat was hurting and so she couldn't go to school. We both knew that pain in the throat or vocal cords, angina, or anything that comes up around the neck chakra is connected with our communication or noncommunication, as the case may be. I asked her what she didn't say but wanted to or said but didn't want to. She replied that she didn't care about that; she just wanted to stay home because she had an exam that day. "Aha," I said with understanding, "why didn't you say so right away?" We both laughed, her throat stopped hurting, and she went to school. Sometimes a little bit is enough. If we just notice and admit what's going on, we wouldn't have to have a problem anymore.

If we don't admit a problem, we can't solve it!

Sometimes we work on our disease for a long time before it finally manifests. Our body can withstand a lot. Suppressed emotions, which we have learned to hide, are a big problem in our lives. After a while, we can't make sense of them ourselves, and we don't know how we feel anymore. I hear very often, "I had a bad feeling, but I don't know if it's right"—they mean the feeling, if it is right. They doubt. We have disconnected ourselves from ourselves, and we think that someone else will know better how we feel. How is it possible that we have forgotten that feelings can't be good or bad? They simply are—and we have them.

If we admit how we feel and we don't like it, we can change it!

But admitting how we feel is something we don't want to do most of the time because we have other things to worry about. We worry about what others will say about the expression of our feelings, how they will judge us, and finally, how we will judge ourselves. How did this happen? Why are we afraid to defend our feelings from other people and from ourselves? Why do we give priority to holding back our so-called bad feeling? And so we become apathetic toward ourselves and, over time, toward others as well.

If we suppress our real feelings, then we aren't capable of action. We lose our power, and so we don't recognize that it is possible that pain will come.

If we noticed our feelings and worked with them, we wouldn't be in pain and we wouldn't be sick. Our feeling would force us to do something, to take care of ourselves. And if our feeling isn't right? Where have all these doubts about the "correctness" of our feelings come from? What sense does the question—right or wrong feeling—have? The only thing we can ask is whether we have it or not, and after, whether it belongs or not.

There are no such things as good or bad feelings, because feelings simply are—and so we feel them.

It may have happened like this: Mom and Dad are taking their little girl on a little trip. They aren't planning to be away for long, so they didn't bring any food with them. Mommy tells the little girl to eat a lot now before they go because in the woods there won't be much food. The little girl isn't very hungry, and because children don't think about the future, she only eats a little bit. They are walking and walking in the woods. After some time, the little girl gets hungry, and so she tells her mom that she is hungry. "But you can't be hungry," says Mom. "You just ate!" Mom makes a threatening face because she is uncomfortable with the little girl's feeling; she doesn't have any food for her after all. The child is confused. *My stomach says that I am hungry, but THEY say that I'm not. So what's up?* We want them to love us; we want to be accepted and to be close to them. We don't want them to be angry with us. We want to be IN UNITY with them. And so we choose to believe the adults, either out of fear or else we truly believe them, thinking that they know better than we do ourselves.

Or "Mom, this sweater itches," complains a child in his new outfit. "Don't make things up. Grandma made that for you, it's made from real sheep's wool." Or perhaps, "It can't itch you, what would Grandma say?" The child is confused. *What is really going on?* Over time, we get used to the idea that our parents know better than we do: what we feel, what we should feel, what we are supposed to think, and later, what we are supposed to say. At the beginning we don't like this at all, but after some time, we get used to it, and what's more, we begin to require them to advise us and decide for us. In this way, by giving up our feelings, we give up our own power. "Mom, I want to go out with the kids"; it pulls us outside. "And you would leave your mother here all alone? You wouldn't do that, Mom would sit here and cry" and so on. So is that a good thing or a bad thing? What do you think?

And because we are slowly giving up our feelings, because we aren't sure whether we will be accepted with these feelings, we learn to push them down or hide them. Some people, in their belief systems, even go so far as to believe that children don't understand anything, that they can't relate, and so they don't feel anything. That's why we decide that in some situations, it is better not to have feelings, because we find ourselves in situations that are unacceptable for us.

If we give up our feelings, we also give up our power.

I used to work sometimes at a home for disabled children. The nurse would choose one particularly sad child with whom they wanted me to work. This particular child was four years old but behaving at the level of a one-year-old. What's more, he didn't react to impulses from the outside world at all; he simply stared in front of himself and behaved disinterestedly. His name was Martin, and he was taken from his parents because they abused him. After a few sessions, he slowly began to express himself. He didn't just stare straight ahead anymore but he started to react to the world around him. However, he also became aggressive toward the other children. Martin had given up his feelings because he couldn't prevent the suffering that he went through while living with his parents. Thus, his first reaction that came up was the aggression, which he had previously suppressed. I was very glad that he had finally expressed himself. But the nurses didn't like his behavior, so they didn't want me to work with him anymore.

The body as a symbol . . . and the meanings of our sicknesses are symbolic too.

Chapter 4

_⸺_

The Body as Symbol

As we think, so our body feels! Our sickness is the consequence of our unbalanced thinking, by which we are destroying ourselves.

The meanings of our sicknesses are symbolic. Each part of our body is symbolic, and it always characterizes some specific function of the body.

Learn your body's language because it speaks to you every second.

Negative thought blocks energy in the body. Our thoughts are sent from our brain, and the brain controls our whole body. All our problems expressed in physical form are reflections of our thinking.

When we have a psychological problem for a long time, which we don't take care of, after a certain time, it becomes projected into our body as well. If we block energy in one area, an imbalance is created, which is expressed as pain. According to the type of negative thinking it is—for example, if we feel angry, hostile, ill-tempered, afraid of loss, if we have feelings of guilt, if we are indifferent, abandoned—each state is manifested in a certain part of our body.

One wonderful way to map these connections is the method of ONE BRAIN, where, through the Behavioral Barometer mapped on a body, you can understand on which parts of the body and in which ways certain kinds of destructive feelings are expressed.

Generally, the meaning of sicknesses works the same for all people, but each of us has our own specific story here as well. So often, because we can't see a solution, or we aren't able to look at the situation differently, we end up damaging ourselves. Our body is always giving us feedback about how this is becoming materialized, what we are in fact doing, and how we are thinking. If we understand and change our behavior, the symptom usually disappears or gradually gets better. The more our body is damaged, the more serious and long term is our sickness, the more we have to come to understand our destruction. And how do we know that we have understood? When the symptoms go away and are not repeated . . .

How wonderful it is to observe everything around us and to come to understand all the connections! How wonderful it is to learn from them!

Once I was in the hospital. It was right after the time when I had caused the car accident, which I already spoke about. I was in the hospital for seven days. I had broken my nose and ribs. At first I couldn't move very much, but over time, I understood the connections more and more and made new decisions, then everything got better quickly. I was staying in Pod Petřínem Hospital. There they have nuns who work as nurses. After a while (I had lots of time), I discovered something about one of the nuns, one who was especially industrious, was almost always in our room and was always helping someone. When she was away, one woman told me that the nun was not working at the hospital, but she herself was there for an operation. I was a little surprised, and I began to be interested in her. Why is she doing that? I asked myself, "What's wrong with her?" Why isn't she concerned with herself at all? She was so unnaturally eager, which most of the time means that someone doesn't think highly enough of themselves. Soon I got the answer. She had come in for an operation on her hands—she didn't have feeling in them; they tingled and didn't get enough blood. Her vessels were clogging up, and her hands were refusing to do their work. It all made sense.

What do our hands mean? Our hands are our tools of action; with their help, we reach our goal. We are what we do! Those are our hands, and so we need to use them first and foremost for ourselves, for our lives, for our creation, for fulfilling our desires, for expressing ourselves—they are our basic tools. Once, as I lay in bed, that particular nun came over to me. "Mrs. Jordan, I'll close the window. You're about to wash, and you'll be cold," she said matter-of-factly, and of course, she went right away to close the window. I was surprised—I had no intention of bathing because I couldn't do it, and I didn't want the window closed at all because I was breathing better with it open. After a while, I understood. What is left for people who never stand up for themselves, who never do anything for themselves, but sometimes still want something? The only thing left for them to do is to manipulate their environment so that it wants what they want, and it appears that they don't have anything to do with it at all. They get their own way through others while pretending that they don't want anything. That's how it was with this nun. She wasn't capable of being the least bit important enough for herself in order for her to be able to close the window simply because she wanted to. I understood that she was the one who really wanted to close the window and to bathe, because she was the one who was going for an operation soon. "Too bad," I exhaled, "but you can close the window if you want to wash—make yourself comfortable." She looked at me, astonished. "Me? No, I don't need to, it's you," she stuttered. I looked at her resolutely, not wanting to hear any more. She looked away. "Well, if you want, I'll wash myself."

After a while, the red and pockmarked rector came to see her. I half heard his monologue to her about how she would be helped but that she must try even harder to serve those around her and she will be forgiven, if she thinks about herself even less and even more about the others . . .

So **our hands!** What are you grasping? What do you not do for yourself, serving others instead? Why aren't you important to yourself? Why do you forget that you serve others the best by expressing your own potential and your uniqueness? That is the true service to humanity.

Our nails! Why do you not stand up for yourself and get rid of your ability to defend yourself? Nails are a symbol of aggression. Glued-on fingernails are today very fashionable for women. It is a wonderful symbol of the process of balancing the value of men and women—the process of equality—when the superiority of men and subordination of women are still big problems on our planet. It is a process of women taking up their own power and taking care of themselves. Nails are for now still artificial, but I believe that all women will come to recognize the equality of both sexes, end their dependence on men, and that a perfect cooperation will be established. Biting one's nails symbolizes lack of ability or desire to defend oneself.

Our legs! Are you going the right direction? Are you stepping forward straight toward your plans, or standing in place? If you have a problem with your legs, if you can't walk, you are immobile and can't move forward. **Our thighs** are our quick reactors, **our shins** are about guilt feelings that we have and why we can't move on, and **our ankles** are our inflexibility. If we have a sprain, it means that we aren't able to adapt our movement to the conditions we have, and we aren't tuned in enough to the world around us. This symbolizes an unwillingness to change our attitude in certain situations. Any kind of pain while walking symbolizes our pain in life—the way we move symbolizes the way we think. **Our knees** are our self-confidence or, when we have problems with them, really more the lack of self-confidence. What about our **toes**, especially our **big toes?** They are the first thing to step in our chosen direction, or not. Perhaps our ingrown toenails give us pain and inhibit movement. Sometimes it is very difficult to assert one's own direction. **The soles** of our feet, our grounding, what do we cut ourselves off from in our lives? **The way we walk** expresses the way we live. Our posture symbolizes our attitude toward life, toward ourselves. Feet turned in means we are closed; open means we are too open, disconnected from ourselves, etc.

What about our **digestion?** Our pains in the stomach, nausea. What can't we digest in our lives? Who or what is bothering you?

What can't you accept? The solar plexus area gives us a message about whether we are able or unable to connect our inner world with the world around us. Don't believe that if your stomach hurts, food is to blame. The food is only helping you to understand your state. Even if you did eat something bad, you didn't do it by accident, because it is always connected with an external situation and your attitude toward it.

Our eyes! A big theme for many people. Any kind of problem with the eyes is about what we don't want to see in our lives, what we don't want to look at. The problem of nearsightedness is fear of the future. Farsightedness means unwillingness to have a close look at some things. Being cross-eyed, we don't see our goal directly, we experience conflict in our decisions, and we don't follow our path directly. Colorblindness is a lack of happiness in life—suppressing emotion and too little activity. Pressure in our eyes is our inner pressure, which we are continuously putting on ourselves.

Our spine! The support of our life, the axis that holds our entire body. It symbolizes a clear direction in terms of our goals, and any misshapenness is a sign of our problems with making comparisons, with expectations, with feelings of low self-worth, and with problems of competitiveness. Whenever we have a feeling that we haven't held our ground or haven't fulfilled our or others' expectations, most of the time, a problem with the spine appears. Stop making comparisons with others; love yourself, go your own way, and your back will not hurt.

Do you have a **stiff neck?** Where don't you want to look in your life? Why don't you change your position and look at things a little differently. The more perspectives we are able to see, the more flexibly we can react in our lives. Life is fun!

Headache. **Our head!** For some people, it is a lifelong theme resulting in eternal dependence on pills. But a little bit is enough— stop punishing yourself for anything. Stop using the self-punishment mechanism on your life's journey, because in every moment in our lives, we are behaving in the best way we know. Migraines are very common when sufferers set themselves aside from life for a while. Pain, that is, their self-punishment, is so great that they can see nothing and no one. Some sources call the migraine the "orgasm of the head," and it appears most frequently in women in connection with unfulfilled sexuality. It is a problem that is easily solved once we understand why we have it.

Heart. Not enough self-love. People who suffer from heart disease are always people who don't believe that they can get love in their lives or who don't believe that they are good enough and don't know that suffering isn't a required part of their lives. They usually suppress their feelings and their wishes.

Lungs and breath related. Breath is life itself. It symbolizes our communication with the outside world, how we exchange energy with other people, how we allow ourselves to express ourselves. The size of our in-breath is a question of self-confidence. Some people hardly breathe at all in their lives you could say they are almost suffocating. Any kind of problem with breathing symbolizes that we are 'suffocating' ourselves—we don't allow ourselves to breathe. So enjoy your life, because it will be what you make of it.

Elimination. With this body function, we get rid of all the unnecessary things, the things that don't serve us anymore. If you have a problem with elimination (constipation, hemorrhoids, etc.), it means that you don't want to get rid of things in your life that no longer serve you and you keep in your life the old junk from past relationships and attitudes, which already showed themselves to be nonfunctional. Why do you fear changes in your life so much? Getting rid of the old always symbolizes the coming of the new, and there is nothing to fear.

What about your **shoulders**? What kind of weight do you carry with them? Get rid of everything that isn't working for your life. Don't accept others' loads, and be yourself.

What about your **ears**? What and why do you not want to hear in your life? Once, an older woman who wanted to hear better came to me. She said that it really bothered her that she is hard of hearing, and she wanted it to change. We began to work. I explained to her that we have problems with hearing when there are certain things in our lives that we don't know how to solve, or we feel that we can't solve, and so we behave as if we don't hear them. Most of the time, this is related to someone in our lives whom we don't want to listen to, or some kind of information we have a problem with. It works for a while, but this escape from solving things after a while begins to express itself as a real hearing problem. If we solve the problem, then we can hear about it, and we don't have to have a problem with our hearing. The older woman nodded knowingly; it appeared that she understood. I asked her what in her life it was that she didn't want to hear. She thought for a bit then blurted out, "Of course, my husband! He is impossible to listen to. I simply don't listen to him anymore."

"So you'll have to change that," I said. "Otherwise, you won't get your hearing back."

"No way. I am not going to listen to him, that's the only way for me to survive. I just don't listen to him anymore. I have tried it, and it would drive me completely crazy. Doctor, you don't know him, but if you did, you wouldn't listen to him either!"

"So ma'am . . . I understand, but in that case, there is no other way. Your non-listening is your survival mechanism."

And what about our **skin**? The skin is actually the body's largest organ. It has the biggest surface area, and it facilitates our connection with the outside world. It makes up our border, where we separate from other people, but it is also where we meet. Our skin reveals all the feelings that we suppress. Think of blushing, of adolescent acne, or of psoriasis, which protects us from an unfavorable external atmosphere, which is a kind of thick hippo skin so we can't be hurt and won't feel pain. Most people who have psoriasis are very hard to work with because they have strongly suppressed emotions, which are precisely what returns us back to ourselves. There is a similar principle at work there as in **overweight** people. People who carry around a lot of extra pounds create the image of being relaxed people for whom things are "no problem." These pounds create a kind of protective armor, which gives them an artificial barrier from the outside world. Sometimes it is very difficult for them to lose weight because their protective programs won't let them. First, it is important to get rid of the fear—the reason why the barrier was built—then most of the time, they can lose weight. People who have excessive appetites have been using food as a substitute to experience fulfillment in their lives, denying real fulfillment. Begin to appreciate your beautiful body. Don't be afraid. Find out why you don't believe in yourself, and you won't have to excessively protect yourself anymore.

Our communication—**our speech organs, throat, tonsils.** If you have angina, ask yourself what you didn't say but wanted to, or perhaps said but didn't want to. What do you hold inside yourself and retain? Why don't you take seriously your right to express yourself freely? Once, I worked with a little girl who had very bad angina. She was prescribed antibiotics, but her mother brought her to me before she started to use them. What if the problem was solvable another way? We had success in figuring out what the girl wasn't saying when she didn't express herself. The problem was that the girl's father was traveling a lot and was not home often. The girl felt rejected by her father, and she didn't express her wishes because she believed that they wouldn't be fulfilled by him. Her mother and I were excited. The little girl accepted the solution so readily that two hours after their visit, they called with the news that her tonsils were completely clear. We have so much power over our lives—how wonderful we are.

If we don't solve the problem of us not expressing ourselves, the problem goes deeper and deeper into our bodies. The next in line in this case is the **thyroid gland,** which, when we have a problem with it, signals that this is a big theme for us in our lives. Our keeping quiet has become chronic, and we have been damaging ourselves with this for a long time. Express yourselves! Realize your importance!

If we continue in this self-destruction, in this process of not expressing one's self, most of the time, the next affected area is the **liver.** Our immune system stops working because we have stopped using it. We start to feel threatened by the outside world because we don't take care of ourselves. The world ceases to be a safe place for us. Understand that you are just as valuable as everyone else and that no one wants to hurt you, unless you are constantly calling forth this hurt yourself by feeling like a potential victim all the time.

And what about sex, and everything that goes with it? The **female organs** and the related frequent problems, from various inflammations, discharges, including operations that remove ovaries, wombs, and everything else? Why do women deny their femininity and endless creativity and feel so much guilt for their sense of fulfillment? Why do they stay in relationships where they aren't loved and they don't get enough love? Be yourselves and create. Love and don't make it a problem.

Friends, there is a lot that I could name, because everything has its reason and meaning. Everything is understandable and therefore changeable. A sick gallbladder is suppressed and unexpressed anger. Diabetes is the constant feeling that nobody likes you. Cancer is also long-suppressed anger turned inward. Varicose veins are connected with not being able to say no and constantly feeling overworked. You will always find an answer.

Sometimes you hear the opinion, "Well, my mom had varicose veins, my grandmother too, and I got them from them. It's inherited, etc." What if it was more like this: If your mom had varicose veins, it meant that she thought too little of herself and wasn't able to say no. She did a lot of things she didn't want to do, and the varicose veins were the result of that. Her mother, who made the same mistakes, was the one who taught her this life attitude, and of course, they had the same problems expressed in their bodies, varicose veins. And what about her daughter? Speculate for yourselves.

In my counseling office, miracles sometimes happen, but sometimes not. Everything depends on each of you, on how you want to live. You can get the answer in every step—all sorts of people know. Just listen! Take responsibility and use the renewing powers of your body and change your thinking. If you understand your sickness, and change your behavior, you don't have to be sick anymore. Even if your sickness is quite serious, don't be afraid to come to understand all the connections. Don't look for a panacea, but put everything together, because . . .

your body and its condition are a perfect symbol of all your thoughts! Love it—and take care of it lovingly!

Chapter 5

_____

The Animals in Our Lives

Have you ever seen dog owners taking their four-legged friends for a walk and had the feeling that they are quite similar? They even had the same expressions on their faces, similar movements—not that the dog owners were walking on all fours, but there was an unmistakably similar energy in their movements. Some move very slowly and deliberately, both dog and owner. Others run around like mad, and it isn't clear who is walking whom.

Our pets, just like everything else around us, reflect our energy and show us ourselves. Of course they are living creatures, but their life goal is very simple: to survive. They do it, surviving in any circumstances we create for them. They adapt to their life conditions in the best way that they can. Because of this, they are capable, through their behavior, of telling us many things about our conscious and subconscious intentions—on whose basis they behave (whether we like it or not).

Our most common personal reporters are probably our dogs. I see it every day with our mail carrier. Well, actually, there are two of them. The first one is very friendly to dogs, and we see her all the time with her arms through the fence, petting our dogs. We have a dachshund, a very intelligent and almost-talking dog, and two shepherds (both female), who are very friendly and have never hurt another animal or a human. When the mail lady has pet the dogs enough, she then gets on her bike and goes on with her deliveries. The second mail lady is a bigger problem. If she sees me in the garden, she shouts from far away, "Close up those dogs, especially that little stinker, they will be after me!" "Don't be afraid," I try to joke with her. "They have already had breakfast, so you don't have to be afraid, they won't do anything to you." But it is a waste of breath, because a lecture always follows directly about how it is crystal clear that all dogs have only one aim in life—to get a bite of the mail carrier and preferably of her personally. It's interesting to watch the dogs at these moments, standing there as if they're just waiting for orders to go for it. The worst is Jonik, the dachshund, because he looks as if he could bite through the gate. He is barking like crazy, with his snout pulled back, behaving in exactly the way our mail carrier was expecting him to. He is a very friendly dog, used to lots of people and children brought around, and I consider him to be a totally reliable animal. Even so, one time, the mail lady complained that Jonik bit her. It's true that he does manage to slip out by himself sometimes, but would he bite the mail lady? And then I saw it myself; he really did dash after her angrily and bite her by the pants leg, refusing to let go. How strong her intention must have been that she compelled even this dog into action. It would have taken so little for that situation to have not occurred. I don't know how she did it, but it is clear that Jonik behaved according to what he saw in her eyes.

We come to know our true intention based on the way that animals behave toward us. Just try to get a dog to come when you say in your mind something like this: "You can run around a bit, we've still got time." The dog will come when you have really decided what you want. I remember Mr. Hornicek once told a story about how his dog always listened to him. His trick was to give orders like "Come here, or not"—and it worked every single time.

Those of you who ride horses, perhaps, understand even better. Horses are big animals, many times stronger than humans, but they are very willing to work together with us. They fulfill our intentions emphatically, by showing them to us, because they embody our energy with their movement.

Recently, my daughter and I went out horseback riding. My daughter has been riding since she was ten, and she has her own horse. She finds it endlessly enjoyable, and she has mostly taught herself to ride—by riding. She knows that it is all related to how much a person believes in themselves, and she tells that to me all the time. That day, we were going down a muddy path. Two horses were up in front, and I was on my horse, bringing up the rear. All of a sudden, we came upon a huge puddle, which took up the whole width of the path. It was bulging with water, of course, but there were other things that could have been hidden under the surface as well. I glared at the puddle, not wanting to go in. *There are so many things we could step on,* I told myself. Still, I prompted my horse to go on, but the horse understood. He froze and wouldn't move an inch. The two riders were disappearing in the fog when my daughter turned and called, "Mom, do you want to go through the puddle or not?" Aha, of course, I understood everything. The horse snorted and walked through the puddle.

Our meetings with certain animals, species, and individuals with certain typical temperaments aren't by chance. I remember how once there was a rabid dog running around our town. He was a vicious wolfhound, and he had been attacking people on the street. The police had been trying for some time to capture the dog without success. At the same time, there was a strange person running around our town who was also attacking people on the street. He wasn't biting anyone, but no one could pass by him without him commenting about something. He was always acting crazy and angry at the whole world and annoying everyone with his urgent speeches. Considering that we pull into our lives everything that has vibrations similar to our own, soon there was news going around that the dog had been killed, run over by an automobile that was driven by . . . guess WHO.

Animals as species have certain characteristic traits, and they can therefore be significant symbols in our lives, or for one of our life tasks. We can take advantage of so much wonderful information if we remember which animals fascinated us as children and which animals we met with during special moments in our lives. To know the animals that we fear or are disgusting to us is important information as well.

People often come to see me because they are allergic to a particular animal. The most typical cases are cats, but also other small, furry animals. All these animals have one thing in common: their contact, touch, with which they bless us. And especially with cats, we get it whether we want it or not. They are a symbol of caressing and touching, and that is a problem of our times in so many ways. If we have problems with caressing and touching, the easy solution is to blame the fuzzy little creatures and banish them from our lives because we are allergic to them. But in reality, it is only a stand-in problem, because the cause is a lack of love, which is usually expressed in a physical fashion. In childhood, it is the frequent and loving touch, caressing with perfect acceptance and expressed pleasure with the proper people (such as our parents); later it is sex with a partner whom we truly love.

Once, a very nice young man who was allergic to cats came to see me. He could barely look at them without his eyes beginning to swell and everything itching. He blew his nose, sneezed, and got all nervous. I have a white cat at home that is interested mostly in those people who come in with this problem. He senses them from far away and immediately goes to pay attention to them. All animals of course long for balance and acceptance, and they will gladly show us our problem—unlike us, they know that they don't have anything to do with it. When I saw what state the young man was in (because it is very hard to completely avoid cats in this life), I sent the cat a message that this time he should leave off with his jokes because the young man was so miserable already. We put together all the connections from his life and worked on a solution together. As I expected, he had problems with physical contact with women because he kept picking types with whom he didn't get what he longed for. In order for us to understand our connections, we should find a story from our lives when we went through a certain situation that we didn't like very much, in reaction to which, we made some kind of decision. With this young man, we chose the last phase of birth—at the time when the doctor had him in his rubber-gloved hand, and the young man shook with resistance. Everything was rough and somehow hitched, and it was exactly the same way later in his life. He imagined his first ever contact would be different. The problem was that he later came to identify with insufficiency, and what's more, he began to create insufficiency in his life. If we expect to have a problem, then we are creating it with our expectation. Everything matched up wonderfully, and we ended the session with a miraculous "I don't have to anymore." The young man smiled, and our white cat waited sympathetically at the gate in order to test him a little by rubbing against his leg. The young man hesitated a moment, then petted the cat and went on his way.

Spiders and snakes have similar symbolic meaning in our lives. They symbolize touch, which frightens us because it is actually forbidden, and this touch is typical for these animals.

You should notice everything that you react to, because the problem isn't in the animal or the situation, but in our reaction to them.

I love animals and the symbols they bring to our lives. Every nation, every culture, each region has its own special typical animal. It is not just that the animals are simply there locally, but they are there because of . . . The Indians gained enormous strength from their use of totem animals. Directly magical concentrations of specific abilities typical for certain animals protected them in certain situations and showed them solutions. They learned to solve their life problems through the animals' characteristics.

We can use this information even today. Recently, the book *Totem Animals* by Mrs. Flášarová and Mrs. Housnarová was published in the Czech Republic. It contains a very well worked-out description of the symbolic meaning of animal characteristics. There are twenty-eight animals with their typical characteristics presented, which you can use on your path toward your goal and toward self-knowledge. There are also cards available with which you can find the animal that can advise you now about something that you need to learn.

Once, I organized a weeklong course in self-knowledge, where we worked with totem animals. Everyone created their personal totem as a symbol of their continuing journey toward success. We carved the animals from linden wood and materialized those qualities into them, which we needed to bring into our lives. The week was full of discoveries and emotions taking their course in connection with the animals in all of us. Some people accepted their totem animal right away and began to carve them with love; others didn't like their totem animal. I remember a friend who had the totem, the rooster. He had to work for a long time to accept the "stupid animal." "Me and a cock, you must be kidding," he fumed but eventually figured out what to learn from this beautiful animal: instant reactions, decisive behavior, simply not to fear, and to go for it. He can achieve great success by learning to use these cock principles in his life, because according to the aforementioned book, the cock is the "prophet of the rising sun." The cock symbolizes unambiguous action and a desire for life, motivation, and joy. No big deliberations—the morning is here and the sun is rising, no foot-dragging . . . What do you make of that, dear friend?

Another one of my friends got some amazing information from her totem animal—she had just left her rented apartment, where she had left everything that she owned with her ex-boyfriend. She was thirty-three years old and had absolutely nothing. She didn't have a place to go, and with empty hands, she began to think, *How did this happen?* Can you guess what totem animal we found for her life and success? It was the beaver, my friends, the beaver, because the beaver is the builder of impregnable palaces and symbolizes the principle of home, cooperation, and safety.

Accept animals into your life and gain from them their wisdom—believe that they will always find you when you need their advice.

Chapter 6

_C‿C_

Do It!

Toward the end of a year, or during our significant anniversaries, we take inventory of our lives. We are compelled to judge whether we have done all we wanted to. Many of us get nervous at these times because we know that what we resolved, we have not achieved. It's time to balance the accounts and begin again. Most of us feel that something needs to change—sometimes fundamentally. It is time to move on.

We were born into the material world. Our body is material, and everything that we create is always expressed in this material world. The basic tools of human creativity are **thought, word, and action.** Everything we come into contact with in this world, everything around us, originated as thought, which was then spoken and ultimately enacted. It is action, of course, that is the most externalized, because

we are what we do!

We can think about ourselves whatever we want. We can tell other people what we're about, what our plans are, etc., but what everyone sees is what we have done, or haven't done as the case may be. For example, "That's the person who invented the wheelbarrow,"

"That's the one who always comes late," "That one bakes great cakes," "That's the one who can't sleep at night," and maybe, "That's the one who's always talking but doesn't do anything." Only through our actions can we move on, because only then can we really recognize if what we have done makes sense. Only through actions can we experience reaction and then decide whether to continue in this way or not. Only through actions can we draw other contexts into our lives. Only by going to meet what we want through our actions—we concentrate our energy through our attention and doing—can we proceed.

If it occurs to you that you want to do something, then simply go ahead and do it!

Almost everyone has seen this happen: you have an impulse to call a certain someone, and if you did it right away, you hear on the other line, "I am so glad you are calling! I was just thinking about you . . ." But if you didn't make that call, then when you finally got around to it, the person was at lunch, then at a meeting . . . and then the next day, had the day off, and so on. Thought is energy, and everyone can feel it on some level—everyone is tuned in.

Often we are surprised by our thoughts, and sometimes we react to an idea as if it were attacking us. We feel threatened by our own idea, such as "I'd like a new car." And our reaction is "Where the hell am I going to get that kind of money?" Why? Why do we judge our ideas as soon as they are born? When we have the thought, there is no way to know what its realization could be. It is an idea that we make material over time. When we decide to have a child, the decision takes place first, and everyone understands that it then takes a minimum of nine months until we see the child. Not until then can we play with or take our creation in hand. Every seed must germinate—and it is important to keep watering too. Be thankful for your ideas. Water them regularly, and they will grow and become material. Be patient but consistent!

Once, I read some advice from a rich banker who said that the secret to success lies in not giving yourself unreachable goals. He makes certain to always give himself goals that he knows he can easily achieve. For example, he would never promise to bring twenty bricks per day out from the garden because he knows that he wouldn't do it, and even if he wanted to, it would be a huge pain in the neck. On the other hand, he knows that he is definitely capable of taking, every time he goes by, one brick and bringing it up to the gate. This plan is realistic for him, and he is able to stick to it. And if he decides he will do it, then he really does it! And things are set in motion.

So good luck with your year-end taking of accounts, and if you want to make a change . . .

simply do it!

Chapter 7

_GD GD_

It's Never Too Late

We often get so used to our problems that it seems to us nearly impossible to change anything. The longer we avoid dealing with things and remain in an inappropriate situation, the more we paralyze ourselves and give up our own power and emotions. The route back becomes so complicated that it can seem as if there's no way back. We identify with our problems and get the feeling that letting go of them would mean giving up our lives.

"You can't teach an old dog new tricks," Michal Tučný[3] sings. Many people have come to cherish this sort of attitude toward their lives. Of course, the time in our lives when we see ourselves as "old dogs" is very individual. Some people feel that way in their sixties, others in their twenties. Back when I still lived with my now ex-husband, there came a time when I began to understand that our relationship needed some fundamental changes. He was symbolically, endlessly, and completely stuck playing Tučný's song. Only fundamental changes could have saved our relationship, but thanks to that song, I was able to understand the situation. Seeing as I didn't feel like an old dog, I soon left the relationship.

---

[3]   Translator's note: Michal Tučný is the celebrated singer of the Czech country and western group Greenhorns.

44

We often put off a clear decision and rationalize why we remain in the same unsatisfying situation. Most often we use "**if**": "If only I had decided differently back then, what can I do with this mess now?" "If I hadn't broken up with Joe, I could still be with him now." Or "If I hadn't had fallen into that creek, I wouldn't have had to dry out those things, which means I wouldn't have met Frank . . . or maybe it's really the storm's fault." "If it hadn't rained, we would have taken a different route, etc." "If I had listened to my parents back then and studied harder . . . but what can I do now?" "If I had gone to a different school, etc." "If "ifs" and "buts" were candy and nuts, we'd all have a merry Christmas." Ring a bell? The decision is done and gone. The past is history. You're living in the present moment, so that's why you have to act in the present moment. Assess the current situation created by your past decisions and decide to act. If what you've created doesn't satisfy you, do something about it.

"If I had only . . ." is something that no longer exists—don't give it your energy.

We often hear "I'm too old for that." "That's not for me anymore." "It's not worth the worry." Some people so systematically reject any sort of change for the better in their lives that they become immobile. Some people become walking corpses, with no meaning in their lives and no possibility of achieving anything. Every lived second influences how and when we die. Elderly people who can't move enough for whatever reason experience the same sort of immobility in their brains. What happens in our brains materializes itself in our bodies. Put simply, they can't move forward in their lives. They no longer believe that they can change anything. They lack motivation and the desire to do anything about it. This doesn't happen from one day to the next, but when we fail to deal with things again and again, we gradually get the feeling that nothing will ever work, and we give up.

Everything that we've lost in our lives, we can usually somehow renew. The only one thing we can't get back is time, which we irreversibly lose by not doing what we want—or for that matter, by not doing things through which we continue to develop.

I'll tell you a story that I'll never forget. I deeply respect this one elderly woman who gave me one of the most amazing pieces of information in my life—namely, that **it's never too late!**

One day, the telephone rang. It was an elderly lady from Moravia. She lived in a village near the town of Znojmo, and she was calling from a telephone booth. She made an appointment with me. It was winter, with lots of snow and ice on the roads. She traveled the whole day, taking many different modes of transportation until, all of a sudden, there she was, standing at our front gate. She had crutches. She was well over seventy years old. I admired her achievement and the energy she invested into her plans. I was looking forward to her story. It was rather modest. Grandpa, that is, her husband, restricted her life a lot. She felt constrained and unable to defy him. He had even attacked her physically a number of times, so she was afraid of him. We found a story from her childhood that was influencing her current life: she had spent her entire childhood looking after her younger siblings, thereby making up for her parents' problem of not having enough time for their kids. Her husband burdened her so much with his own problems that it was nearly impossible for her to leave the house. The fact of the matter was that by taking care of her husband, she was continuing to take care of her younger siblings.

However, the old lady had her own dream. She dreamed of going to Medjugorje, the well-known pilgrimage site in Bosnia-Herzegovina, but she never dared speak about it in front of her husband. After we successfully unblocked her, she realized that she was free. She was free to make her own decisions; others would have power over her only to the degree to which she allowed it. She left. Two weeks later, my son informed me, "Mom, that granny from Znojmo called and said that I should tell you that she doesn't need her crutches anymore." I received a postcard from Medjugorje that summer.

Another very common excuse for not dealing with an unsatisfactory situation, for example, in relationships, is our children. They tend to be the fictitious reason why we stay in a relationship that doesn't bring us any happiness. "Why don't you divorce him? Why are you still with him? Come on, what do you get out of it? He doesn't give you any money, he's never home, he is a drunkard, he treats you

hideously . . . I don't understand you," our friends ask incredulously. And the woman in question responds completely seriously, "I'm doing it because of the kids. You know, I can't take their father away from them." Dear friends, listen to what you're saying! Not staying in a relationship with someone you don't love is not going to rob anyone of his or her father! You're not responsible for your partner's relationship with your children, nor for their relationship with him. No child would want you to make that sort of a sacrifice. The only thing you'll get out of it is that they will stop respecting you and they will start behaving toward you like your problematic partner does. The only thing you're uncompromisingly teaching your kids by taking that sort of a stance is how to live in unsatisfying relationships and how to live without love. You're giving them instructions on how not to respect themselves and how not to care of their own lives. On top of that, you're fostering a feeling of guilt in them for being the reason you can't leave. Ask yourself, why do you really not want to leave? If you're playing a disingenuous game with yourself, then you're playing it with your children as well. You're teaching them not to trust themselves and how to lose their own self-worth. Your kids know the truth, even though it may not seem like they do.

A good friend of mine told me about how long it took him to decide to break up with his wife. They hadn't been truly living together for a long time, just sharing the same roof, and what's more, under very inhospitable conditions. They had one child. My friend's wife had a drinking problem. He had succumbed to the all-too-common delusion of staying with her because "it's important for a son to be with his mother." However, he forgot that children learn how to live primarily by growing up within the context of a harmonic partnership between two parents. That's how they develop functional models for their future relationships. The situation became untenable, and he finally decided to leave. He spent a lot of time desperately trying to come up with how he would tell his ten-year-old son the news. One day, he made up his mind to tell him. He called him over and began carefully, "What would you say to me if I told you . . ." and then continued, "that I want to leave your mom?"

"So finally!" his son responded and went off to pack his stuff . . .

Chapter 8

_ɔ﹋ɔ_

I Feel Rejected So Often

One of the very consequential tricks we have in our lives—part of the "How Not to Achieve Our Goal" program—is feeling **rejected**. It works because, then, we aren't able to go out and meet things in our lives; we can't attract the right situations because we are afraid of rejection. This perfect tyrant controls our steps and paralyzes us in unexpected moments, when we really want a particular thing, but for some unknown reason, we don't get it. Most of the time, we even know that we are bringing this about ourselves on some level, but we can't help ourselves. But I really wanted it, I really believed, and **it** didn't work out again! Same as always, rejections . . . And again, the magic formula: **"it" keeps on happening to me**.

So, dear rejected ones, take responsibility. Stop blaming the world and start asking yourselves what you are doing to cause this repetitive model, which gradually becomes our main life program and excuse number 1. Some of us develop this to such perfection that we no longer try to do anything because, of course, we know exactly how it will turn out.

This attitude is reflected very strongly in our relationships. We can never feel equal with our partners, because if we are in constant danger of being refused, we feel as though they have infinite power over us. We react to this rejection by trying too hard in our relationships, which over time results again in this well-known rejection—because we stop believing in our own worth. In order not to have problems with a possible rejection, some people behave unpleasantly right away; they get rejection much faster than those who try hard. Our parents frequently teach us about this attitude. "It's best not to get too excited, so if it doesn't work out, then you won't be too disappointed . . ." We take this as practical advice, but we don't realize that much of the time, we turn our expectation of possible failure into an intention of failure—and what we want usually happens.

Remember the joke about Cohen and Goldstein? Goldstein needed to borrow some carrots from Cohen, and he was trying to figure out the best way to ask him; he came up with "Cohen, please can I borrow some carrots?" He thought about it for a bit and decided he didn't like it. *Why should I beg him for it?* he thought. *I'll just tell him, "Cohen, lend me some carrots. Okay."* On his way up to the first floor, he decided he isn't happy with that either. "No, this is better. I will tell him, 'Give me some carrots.'" Satisfied, he continued up to the next floor, but he stopped once again with the thought, *No, I will ring the bell and just tell him, "Carrots."* But he still wasn't happy with how the whole thing was shaping up. Finally he stopped at the fifth floor, where he rang the bell. Cohen opened the door, and Goldstein burst out at him, "Cohen, you can shove those carrots up your ass." And Goldstein walked back down the stairs.

Perfect. It's not a joke, my friends; it's reality, because that is how a large percentage of people behave. So what should we do about it? Aren't you sick and tired of this endless self-rejection?

This whole connection with rejection helped me to disentangle one nice young man who was getting sick of that state. His name was Lou, and he felt rejected often. He felt that his girlfriend was unresponsive and that he was being rejected often, especially when it came to sex. He was unhappy that his girlfriend wasn't more active, and what's more, that she was rejecting his initiatives. Of course, this was Lou's point of view. It was interesting that his girlfriend also felt rejected, but by Lou. Though on the surface this doesn't seems to make sense, there is logic to it, because **when we reject ourselves** by expecting rejection from other people, then actually we give preference to rejection in our relationships with our partners. In order to avoid rejection, we don't get involved in certain activities, and so we don't let the other know that they are important to us. When the fear of rejection is more important for us than what we can get out of the relationship, we reject our partners as well. Our partner can't feel our interest in them, and so again, we get what we want. Rejection . . .

During unblocking sessions with my clients, we often go through situations in their past when they took the rejection model into their lives. A particular situation from their life facilitates our understanding. At first glance, everything may appear quite hopeless because **they** don't want to satisfy our wishes, don't have time for us, don't even want to listen to our request. We try different kinds of manipulations and tricks to get attention in order to reach our goal, but nothing works. Sometimes we even hurt ourselves or break something, so they will finally pay attention to us. We do eventually get some attention, but not the kind that we imagined. During the unblocking sessions, we come to a simple conclusion in most cases:

> **If we said what we wanted, clearly and directly, most of the time we would get it!**

So why don't we do it? It is strange, but for some reason, we don't stand up for what we want. As we have already said,

> **no one does anything they don't want to do. So let's take responsibility!**

Why do you still need to feel that way? That is to say, rejected. Wouldn't it be more pleasant to expect the best and to get it? And what about others, you may ask—they can't always want what we want? Of course, we aren't here alone, and we have to let other people freely decide what they want. The only difference is not to see other people's choices as rejection. We just have a new experience: this isn't the right way to go. Then we can try out new options how to get what we want. Don't create a negative program ahead of time, which other people sense on a subconscious level and then they don't have the least desire to meet your needs. What would you say, for example, about a lady who comes into a grocery store just as they are about to close, saying, "So I guess you don't have bread for me today, right?"

"No, we don't" effortlessly slides out of the salesperson's mouth. Or an exasperated "Why shouldn't we?" Very often we have a habit of avoiding saying concretely what it is we want in social situations. On the street, people ask us conspiratorially, "Do you have a watch?"

"I do," I usually say, and keep on walking. "A little salt wouldn't hurt," says someone visiting me for dinner and expects that I will jump up to bring the salt. Since I don't use much salt, I simply see this as an expression of a different opinion. Friends, if you want some salt, ask for the salt directly! Give your intentions clarity. **Ask and you will receive!**

Chapter 9

Our Boundaries

You could say that every person we meet could be exciting for us. Everyone is fascinating and wonderful in some way. If we happen to be alone with this person or we see them separately from other people, his or her attitudes and opinions can possibly seem to be perfect. Problems can come up, on the other hand, when this particular person comes into contact with other people. We can have a fantastic picture of someone but can be very surprised about their reactions to other people or at the way that he or she behaves. And that's the point—because each of us can be expressed chiefly through other people, because it is precisely through our reactions to other people that we can come to better know ourselves. Our relationships characterize us, and only by the relationships we have in our lives, that is, whom we relate to, do we recognize who we really are.

> **The problem isn't what the other people are doing, but it's that we are reacting to it or how we are reacting.**

Some people completely dissolve and get sublimated out in the world of other people. They are always worried about who said what to them, what someone wanted from them, what someone expected from them, and when they are in confrontation with other people, they always give priority to others before themselves. To the question "Ana, do you want to come over?" They answer, "Well, you know how Joe is . . ." Or to the question "Do you like your job?" We get the answer "My mom said that . . ." and so on. You would never find out from these people what they actually think because they're always worried about what other people might think and whether they themselves were behaving correctly in their relationships with other people. This constant desire to please leads to surrendering oneself, and most of the time, the expected acceptance and appreciation of others don't come, because the "selfish ingrates" can never have enough and will demand more sacrifice. Those whom we are trying to please become our "torturers" most of the time, and we, who put in all the effort, are disappointed and deceived. This is the story of many young women who try to meet their partners' wishes, people whom many times they didn't even want as partners but were unable to say **no**.

Maybe it started like this: "He asked for my phone number. He was a real jerk, and I didn't like him at all. He just kept on bugging me. I was uncomfortable," said a young woman with two young children to me. I was interested, and I asked what happened after that because I supposed that nothing more could happen after that. But something did. "So finally I gave him my phone number," she replied. "But why?" I popped my eyes at her. "So he would stop bothering me," she answered matter-of-factly. I asked her what happened next. "Well, tough guy called me." She was agitated now. And what happened next? "He wanted to meet, the stupid fool."

"And you met with him?"

"Yeah, I met with him. What was I supposed to do? He wouldn't have left me alone. You don't know him, what he's really like," she continued indignantly. Then I stopped being surprised because the rest of the story continued in the same light. Afterward, her new friend asked her if she wanted to sleep with him, and what did she say? What was she supposed to do, could she refuse him now? How would he feel then? So they slept together because there was nothing else to be done. But she didn't want to do it; it was him. Then they started dating, because that's just how it was, and finally they got married because, because, because . . . and then they had kids together, or really I believe it was that he had them with her, because she didn't want them, because everything just "happened" to her. And now she is sitting across from me, this beautiful young woman, full of tears and without direction in her life. She is thirty years old, and maybe now it will finally occur to her that she has to go at it a different way.

Friends, this story is true, and it is far from unique. We use endless variations on this model, and we are still learning about this one core theme in our lives: **our boundaries.**

> **Other people behave toward us in exactly the manner that we let them!**

The other extreme that we see around us in people's behavior every day are the "eternal warriors." They are set up for a fight about anything anytime. Everyone is their potential enemy, and every situation is a provocation for them to fight. They are on guard all the time. Life is a battle. They are in constant confrontations, guarding their boundaries, which other people are "overstepping" all the time, simply just because they exist at all.

Once, I heard a story about an American farm owner who every day walked the boundaries of his land, ready to shoot the first trespasser he saw step on his property. He did this intensively for a year, gun in hand, waiting to see if someone would dare disrespect his boundaries. One day, as he was out on his rounds, he tripped, stepped on the gun, and shot himself . . .

Poor, unlucky guy, you might say. No—this is simply the workings of a universal law. The law of cause and effect is the basic law of our lives, and that is true for both of the cases we discussed above.

And then there is another type, a third, people who think that they can get around it by not dealing with it at all. These are the people who put on their armor and pretend that they don't have any problems with the external world at all. "Everything is just fine, totally cool," they say with a smile. "I can handle it." Most of these mellow people have one thing in common. They gain pound after pound, creating an artificial distance from others, and their "satisfaction" grows and grows. Only their consumption of food grows and grows even though these people often say that they hardly eat at all. But they don't care because they are "just fine." The security of artificial boundaries. They seem to be the tough ones. Other people feel good with them because there is "something to lean on."

And then there are those who are always looking for someone they can lean on. They constantly need someone who will make them feel sure that their decisions are right. Doubters. "How am I supposed to do it? Do you have any advice?" There is always someone who is ready to take responsibility for them, someone whom they can blame if it turns out their advice wasn't so good.

And then (of course) the strong men step up, they who have an answer for every question and always know what "the best" is for each and every one. They are able to give advice in any situation; they just know how to do it. What distinguishes most of these types, however, is that the only people they are not able to advise are themselves.

Our boundaries...

There are endless variations on the models played out in our relationships; we use endless models in this endless game about energy that we lose when we aren't in balance, energy that we try to get back again in an unbalanced way. If, however, we want to find out something about ourselves, there is nothing else we can do, because it is the only possible way we can come to know ourselves. People who renounce relationships and who stop communicating with the outside world because they think, for example, that the world is evil or somehow bad—these people stop developing, and they can have the mistaken notion that everything is okay with them. If we feel that something from the outside world is a threat to us, whatever it is, the problem isn't with the outside world but with our own boundaries. We doubt ourselves somewhere, and we don't believe that we will be able to take care of ourselves in a certain situation, or that we will be able to face up to what we fear. It is always important to think about this because

everything that we fear, we pull into our lives.

The goal of the Universe is balance. For example—if we have a fear of criminals, we will probably meet with them in our lives soon, because these beings are very tuned in to take advantage of any crack in our boundaries and to take advantage of every invitation into our lives. If you listen to the news reports about a woman who was attacked and raped in the park, probably very few women are aware that that is the story of one particular woman and not all women. She, that one woman, on the basis of her fears, brought this problem into her life. If we could talk to her, we would probably find out that something similar happened to her or to her mother, who, all through her childhood, warned her never to go into the park or she might get hurt. Our boundaries . . .

We all need to come to know ourselves, primarily by understanding our space, which we can make use of. Our children are the most wonderful teachers about our boundaries. They try everything for such a long time until finally we boil over and express ourselves bluntly—because it wasn't until that moment that our attitude became persuasive. Even in the moment when it seems that we have made everything clear, they try going a little further, and that is a message for us that there is still a little chink in our attitude, which they can take advantage of. Children feel that chink, and they want to be clear about it, to find out if perhaps that space doesn't belong to them. They are very excited about life and their constant research about life, and they are great teachers for us. That's why they are always going right up to our borders, because they want to be sure exactly where they end and where we begin.

Once, a woman came into my counseling room who wanted me to work with her five-year-old daughter. She said that her daughter was badly behaved and terrible, that she embarrassed her, and that they could barely go anywhere together. She said that she herself is a nice lady whom everybody likes. The first person she has had a problem with in her life is her terrible child . . . I asked her if she ever wondered why she, such a wonderful lady, has such an awful child. She quickly jumped past the question and began to tell me a story.

"So just imagine, we are waiting for the trolley car, and the child starts screaming that she doesn't want this trolley, she wants to go in a blue one. The blue one comes, and the child screams again that she wants a red one. Okay, so what can we do? We wait for a red one—who could listen to that screaming? When the red one comes, now she wants a yellow one. Everything now is messed up—we'll be late—I have to do something. Another trolley is coming, and I decide that this time we are getting on it. And what happens next? The little monster lies down on the sidewalk and starts acting completely crazy—people must think that I kidnapped her. Fine—we will wait for the blue trolley, I wanted to satisfy her so she wouldn't scream . . ." Aha, I asked quickly, "You wanted to satisfy her, or you wanted her not to cry?" No answer. The mother continued, "Do something with her!"

So, dear mother! Where has your pride gone? Where is your love for yourself? Where are your boundaries? Your child cannot possibly behave any different until you begin to value yourself and stop allowing your wonderful daughter to run your life. Your child is, on some level, a continuation of yourself, especially when it's a girl. No one can show you this problem of you as perfectly as she can. She slowly started to understand. We looked more into her own childhood, to find where and why she decided to give other people priority over herself and then to blame them for it. Why did she give up her own power and give up her own boundaries?

Why do we retreat from what we find uncomfortable? On the basis of what experience do we think that if we tolerate and overlook what we don't want, other people will stop doing it? Why don't we stand up for ourselves? Why don't we understand that by doing this we are losing our freedom and becoming dependent on the outside world and on everything that we fear?

Whenever you don't stand up for yourself, you lose your power! It's not because THEY are strong—it's because YOU are weak.

We waste a lot of time, for example, explaining to others that things are not how they say they are, and we give reasons and justifications for our behavior. Doing this, we lose a huge amount of energy, everyone feels our insecurity, and our boundaries actually dissolve; and of course, they aren't respected.

Recently, I worked with a friend of mine on her problem of not standing up for herself. It always took her a while to understand that she has missed the right moment to stand up for herself; she realizes it only when she feels badly and other people are taking advantage of her. We did an exercise demonstrating it. "Imagine," I said (to explain a little, my friend has a horse and taught herself to ride. She loves the horse a lot, and she is trying to enjoy communicating with the horse in a way that is slightly different from the usual way—but her doubts about her qualities take her power from her and cause her to have the impression that others are making fun of her), "you are leading the horse out of the barn, and all at once you hear, 'Where are you going with that goat?' What do you do?"

"I laugh and go on."

"Okay, and how do you feel?" I asked. "Pretty bad, I would rather not have run into him."

"And what did you do, that you feel bad? What is it that is bad here?" Seeing as how we ourselves are the source of our own feelings, we need to look inside ourselves to see what caused our bad feeling. We think for a minute. Okay, someone is making some stupid joke, and we just smile at them; that probably wouldn't work, so the problem is her reaction. Let's try a different one . . . What about, "This isn't a goat, it's a horse," she said. "Are you better?" I asked. "No, not much better." Why? Giving reasons. Is it really necessary to explain to this person that her horse isn't a goat? If you overexplain and, as the case may be, try to justify yourself, on some level, you actually admit that it could even possibly be true. In this case, that the horse could be a goat. The whole thing is just a fight for energy, which my friend actually entered, and so far, she is just losing energy because the person in question knows that her horse isn't a goat. Of course, the first example is an option, not to react at all to the silly comment—but she would have to actually feel good about that, that is, really not to react at all, because she is sure what her horse is. But if my girlfriend registered a bad feeling, she has to come out with it—because whatever you suppress turns against you. **Our boundaries.** Attacked by foreign armies. If we don't react, the foreign army pushes on. We played around a little while longer with her story, and finally she told her provocateur, "So say that again, and you'll get it!" She was satisfied. That was the right thing. The boundaries have been defended, and the enemy is retreating. He understood that he can't go there. In reality, no one really wants problems. And now she finally feels really good. She took care of herself. There was nothing to fear.

When we know exactly where our borders are and we are willing to defend them, we will recognize this by the fact that other people respect us instead of doubt and attack our borders. Everyone can then feel perfectly well that we value ourselves. And if we will be firm in our borders, if we will not emanate energy of our doubts, they won't test us. Every situation in our lives is in a way new, so we will most probably be working on our borders for the rest of our lives.

I would like to talk about our boundaries in connection with today's much-discussed theme of bullying. This theme is given particular attention in every school. It is significant because it shows us how our children work with their boundaries, and it informs us of our children's impaired self-esteem, those who bully and those who are bullied. Neither party feels that they are on an equal level with the outside world, and so they have the need to either demean the other or be demeaned. In many cases, this is a process of defining one's own boundaries and standing up for oneself. Children are often capable of being in this mutual game, very unequivocal, uncompromising, and cruel, and they have an ability to sense the smallest chinks in the self-esteem of other children. I think that the problem can often be solved, first of all, on the level of the attitude of the children who are unable to stand up for themselves and who thus provoke the other children to try and see how far the victim will let them go. I think that even from the perspective of classical psychology, the more problematic child is the one who is constantly being hurt by the other children because they have problems with self-esteem, and they learn to get energy from others by letting themselves be hurt. A certain amount of aggression is a normal expression in life, and if the general rules of cooperation or the moral foundations of our society aren't broken, this is less of a problem than the "professional" victim. When working with these kinds of children, we usually work with their parents as well, because the children learned everything they know from them. Often after discussion with the parents, I find out that this victim role of their children actually "suits" them in a very strange way—so thus they learn finally to stand up for their children, because most of the time, they didn't learn to stand up for themselves.

My youngest son, Samuel, once brought a note home from his teacher, saying he was supporting bullying in school. I discussed it with my son, who explained that some of his classmates had peed into another classmate's hat, and other children laughed at him, Sam among them. (Note: Sam was in fifth grade at the time.) The teacher was very unhappy with the situation and punished the onlookers for not stopping it. I understand the teacher's point of view, and it is clear to me why she dealt with the situation that way. Even so, I think that it is a very serious situation for this child who has been degraded like that. My son told me, "Mom, I just don't get how that kid just stood there and watched it. I would have killed those kids if they tried it on me." Our boundaries . . .

When we don't stand up for ourselves, we are admitting on some level that we deserve to be treated this way. Once, I worked with a little girl who had, starting in first grade, problems with boys (from her class, also first graders) who, during breaks, several times pushed her into a corner and pulled down her underwear. This problem was constantly a topic of discussion, and her mother would put on offended expression, blaming everyone. Why did that little girl value herself so little that she allowed that to happen? Something basic was missing in her pride and self-esteem. Why didn't she just stand up for herself? Look for the answer in your childhood, when you didn't get something important and then you identified with that lack of it and with the low self-esteem of your parents. The mother of the girl we were talking about just couldn't get it. It seemed to her that her daughter's problem made her interesting in a strange way, and so she didn't want to change anything. Once, the girl's grandfather came to the session with her, and he understood the problem very quickly. "Why don't you just give 'em a slap, you poor girl?" And so he began having regular "fighting" lessons with the little girl, and soon the problem was solved. The next time it happened, she explained to the boys with her hands what she thought about the situation, and they stopped bothering her. From that time on, it never happened again, and power and joy returned to her life.

However, standing up for oneself openly isn't always the problem. In certain situations, due to the very fact that we know our worth and understand what pride is, we don't react to certain challenges. Because that which we relate to, we become.

Once, my office phone rang, and as I answered it, a male voice began explaining to me that he had read about me in a magazine and would like to meet me. He didn't want anything bad . . . At first I didn't understand. I am used to consulting with people over the telephone about all kinds of problems, so I tried to find out what kind of problem he had. Only, he didn't have a problem. Or certainly not the kind that he would want to solve. He wanted to meet with me for a single very concrete purpose. When I finally understood what he was on about, I explained to him that he should find a better way to find a date, and I asked him if that was really necessary. He still didn't get it. "So where and when?" he asked. All this was a big lesson for me. With my foolish, up-front, and clueless attitude, I really deserved all that I got; he called me regularly at night for three weeks and bothered me. At first I tried to explain things to him, then I tried switching off the phone, but nothing helped. Then I finally realized what I had been doing. The next time he called, I dashed madly for the phone and I cursed at him using the foulest words I knew. I was so angry I almost lost my breath. Angry at whom? At myself, of course. And finally I yelled at him, "You just try calling me again, you—!" I had hit the edge. The army was standing at attention. He never called again.

And now we have reached blackmail. Our own worth. Our boundaries. No one can be blackmailed without their own consent. There must be two for every blackmail. Us and them.

And crime. Every crime needs two parties. Criminals and victims. If there weren't people who were potentially willing to become victims, I believe that criminals would also cease to exist. Let's begin working on the other side of the seesaw as well, because the Universe longs for balance—**the Universe is balance.**

Chapter 10

You Have Your Goal

Two souls meet, and one soul asks, "Do you know how to love?"

"Of course," says the other. "Okay, so I have an idea. Let's go to Earth together, and you can try it out there." And continues, "On Earth they live in material bodies, and so everything that you think happens. You get to find out if you really can do it." The first soul gets all excited about what a great idea it is and is ready to go immediately. "And I," the second soul begins, "will be your soul-friend, and I will go there with you, and I will do the most terrible things to you, things you can't even imagine. And you? You will love me."

"Mm, okay, let's go already." The first soul is in a hurry, looking forward to love, but the soul-friend is still not ready. "Why aren't we going?"

"But there is just one snag," the soul-friend says. "You must never forget who I am . . ." That is kind of how I see it; that's also the way Mr. Walsch writes about it in his *Conversations with God*.

So, friends, now the process of remembering who you are and **what you actually want** begins. Because each of us most likely has a kind of task, which, to some extent, is pregiven to us and known to us on some level. However, everything depends on our choice, of course. We could have been someone completely different from who we are; we could have been a million different people, but we are who we are—one particular sperm and one particular egg, one particular human, one particular **choice**. And it is completely up to us to what extent we fulfill our goals, to what extent we take advantage of our potential on the basis of our life choices. It is completely up to us what kind of life we are going to have, and it is completely up to us how we are able to connect to what is happening in the world around us and express ourselves.

When we are little children, even tiny babies or embryos, we also of course have a choice to decide in certain situations. But it is very difficult to be ourselves if we don't take care of ourselves and if our very existence is dependent on those closest to us. We long for Unity, and we have it hardwired into our brains as a basic principle. That is why it often happens, or it almost always happens, that we give precedence to unity with the outside world and we act against ourselves, behaving exactly like "THEM" even if, on the inside, we don't agree. We make the mistake of thinking that in this way, we will gain unity and the acceptance of the outside world, beginning with our parents. "That girl is going to have problems with her weight like I do, just look at her, Daddy," our mother says and fears that that is what will one day happen. The girl doesn't understand why she should have problems with her weight, but after a while, it just happens. "Our boy will just never be good at school," Father soberly states, and the boy struggles and struggles with his studies. "I told you so," says Father, shaking his head and not understanding the influence he has had on the situation. Some authors classify these parents' negative statements (of course, there are worse ones than this one) in the category of black magic, because children have such little power to refuse and overcome their parents' assertions and expectations. But—of course—we have a choice!

I think about it like this: In the case I decide to be born on Earth, I shall find suitable parents ahead of time. Most of my clients describe it this way, and they follow a similar basic theme. For instance, I want to pursue alternative medicine here on Earth and to connect it with Western medicine, because it's time that people stop bickering about the importance of the one or the other. It is time to understand that truth is in connecting different viewpoints, and if differences exist, it is necessary to bring them together. That is why I will choose parents who will help me to get the information I need and give me two different points of view. So my father—he will be a scientist working, maybe, in cancer research, a very educated person, that's one pole. My mother—she will be a simple but intelligent woman, a herbalist and healer who understands nature and energy, that's the other pole. On some level, all of us have the task of connecting our mother and father aspects in our lives, that is, the left and right hemispheres of our brains. But if we look into our parents' lives, perhaps we see that our father drinks a lot, comes home late, stays in the lab until all hours, and neglects his wife; and Mother, she is afraid of him and is unable to defend her use of herbs in front of him. She leaves them on the last shelf in the cupboard and only uses them when Father isn't home. So what now? Well, that's not what I want to live in at all, we say, even before we are born.

It is up to us to accept the conditions that we have chosen as the perfect ones for our growth and perfect for our overcoming. We are born to specific parents, in a specific place, at a specific time. Often people say, "If I were born in a different time, you know, people had it tough then, today it is much easier." Whenever we don't accept one of the starting conditions of our lives, it is as if we have broken the foundations of a church that we have just built. It is likely that the rest of the building will fall. But we do have the choice to try and see what all can be done with it. We have the choice to use it in the best way we are capable of, because we will get no new foundation stones for our temple.

In order for us to at least partially remember what the real thing is for us, we can look into our childhood. The way we liked to play as children is often closely associated with our journey to our goal, because as children, we still remember various things that we spontaneously want to do. In childhood, we create our dreams, which, as adults, we want to fulfill. Once, I read an interview with Karel Gott.[4] To the question, how does he see his life? He answered,

---

[4]   Translator's note: the Czech and German Frank Sinatra.

"I am singing, **I am living my dream.**" And he is really one of the rare people who see it clearly.

And if it is not clear to us, we will miss it in our lives. At a certain time, most often after the age of forty, we suddenly become nervous, and we start to have a feeling that something indefinite is lacking. We are not satisfied with our own life. It is as if we are missing something that can't be named, and most of the time, this need forces us to do something—that is, some of us.

Once, a man came into my counseling room, complaining that he didn't have a life goal. He already had everything he thought necessary in his life—a small hotel, money, some land. Basically, he didn't lack for anything, but he didn't enjoy anything. He had no taste for life. He was about forty-five years old, and he was very sad. That was exactly **it**, that thing that visits each of us at a certain age. While looking for answers, we went back to the time when he was four years old. He remembered that his parents had sold the horse that he had spent every free minute on, dreaming his dreams, since the age of two. The stable and saddle were his two favorite places in the world. When his parents sold their horse, this for the little boy was the end. I spoke the question to him almost automatically, "Do you have a horse?"

"No," he said. "I never thought of it, but it would be no problem at all for me to get one." A light shone in his eyes. "I'll do it."

Of course, I don't believe that this man will buy a horse and immediately know his life goal, but it is through these activities that bring us joy and fulfill us that we can reach our goal.

So—do what you love!

After creating our dreams and plans in childhood, whether consciously or unconsciously, we arrive in the adult phase. Here, it is our job to know how to take care of ourselves and to get everything that we need into our lives in order to renew our energy and to have a comfortable life according to our individual ideas of it, that is, how we allow ourselves to. This isn't the goal of our lives, as many people think—it is just a foundation in order for us to finally begin to realize our dreams. If we stop in that phase, a feeling of emptiness and unfulfillment comes.

According to the education project "Mandala of Life" by Czech author Helena Vertelmanova-Haladova, the first phase of our life is the "Princess" phase, the phase of dreams and plans but without having responsibility for anything. The second phase, from approximately eighteen to thirty years, is when we learn to take care of ourselves, take responsibility, and acquire enough of a base self-confidence and self-reliance for our lives. This phase is the "Ruler" phase. It is when we understand that we can get everything that we want. The next phase, which we must go through, is a return to our dreams, where sometimes we have to give up some of the comfort that we have achieved, but the end result of this is that we achieve even more. It is the "Student" phase, where we begin to try and find our Princess, that is, our dream . . . Our friend with the horse had to make exactly that step; otherwise, he would live with his feeling of emptiness because the foundations that he had built would otherwise be pointless. We all desire to find this **it**. It is what is important and meaningful for our lives. Because

> **we are what we are doing. Thus, it is one of our activities that will endlessly fulfill us, and through this activity, we will be expressing ourselves in the most wonderful way.**

Every one of our cells has its memory and longs to fulfill the **law of dharma**, which is the purpose of our life. Everyone is unique, and each of us has a unique talent. According to that law, every one of us has his own completely unique way of expressing his talent. At around the age of forty, we should already have a little idea of what it is; otherwise, we often just won't feel good. It doesn't matter if you feel that you don't know. Think about your Princess—your dreams— and just try something. Don't make excuses that it's too late or that you are already old; it is all right to start where you left off at ten years old, when the adults were explaining to you that what you are doing is silly. Because it isn't silly. And the only one who really knows it is you yourself. You will know that you are fulfilling the law of dharma, your life's purpose, when, during a certain activity, you have a feeling of bliss and timelessness and you really become the activity you are doing in that moment. When you have found the purpose of your life, you will be willing to give up all your money just to be able to do it again. The "Wonderworker" phase begins when you know what the "**it**" is for you, but don't forget that you still need to keep going on because **you still have your goal**.

Chapter 11

Our Parents

Whether we like it or not, our parents represent a basic library of instructions affecting our lives.

"I will never do with my children what my mother is doing now," says a ten-year-old girl when she gets slapped for making a sour face about eating soup. But never say never. Time goes on, the little girl grows up, and a little girl is born to her. Her own little girl grows up and is now ten years old. One day she comes home and is hungry. She asks her mom what kind of food she can make for her, and her mother offers her soup. The daughter doesn't like the idea, and so her face shows it—and suddenly, it's here. Mom takes off as a special wind of rage takes over her mind. Her hand shoots out; she doesn't even know how. And the slap has landed in the world. "Don't you make a sour face about my soup," roars Mom, with the same accent and same intensity as her own mother once did.

If everything goes well, we are able to figure out, at least after the fact, which way the wind was blowing. Let's say that when the mother-girl calms down, she is able to say, "What have I done? You know, my mother did that to me, and I said I would never do it to my daughter!" Then she feels guilty, which doesn't help, and she makes a vow that this time really **never** again! But most of the time, it doesn't work, because we use the behavior that we have rejected when we are stressed. In such moments, we are in a state of reduced consciousness. And what we reject in our lives, we are at the same time attracting. The only way to get rid of it is to accept that that is how it was and to not lay blame on anyone anymore because, in the present, we have a choice!

That is very difficult to do because we never know exactly which situations and which principles we have pulled out from the lives of our parents, from our library. What's more, the way we see the whole thing is affected by the suppressed emotions that we felt at the time. We can go deep into our past to times when we noticed our parents' behavior and relationship, and we were able to register each imbalance in their thoughts and attitude. In certain periods, our parents' attitude toward us deeply influences our future attitude toward ourselves. It is a very small percentage of people who come in to the world expected, preaccepted and respected, and importantly, without fear and unreasonable expectations about who or what they should be for their parents' sake.

One of the important periods is when the mother found out that she was pregnant. Once, I worked with a boy who had a strong stutter, so much so that he wasn't able to express one whole thought of his own. His biggest problem was saying his name. He wasn't able to catch his breath at that moment. Finally, we got at the main cause of his problem. When his mother found out she was pregnant with him, she had only one thought—that no one should find out, especially not her father, who didn't like her choice of partner. She was afraid what would happen. She wasn't able to stand up for her choice, not for herself, not for her baby. This huge imbalance influenced the little boy so much that to this day, he is unable to stand up for himself and express himself.

A secret child . . . But let's start from the fact that we chose our parents—so what is this child here on this earth supposed to learn? At first glance, we can see that he must learn to stand up for himself and to express himself. To what extent? Only he himself knows. His mother's keeping him a secret works in this case as a lesson, which he is supposed to overcome and to understand that everything is okay and that he has, right here, his own irreplaceable place. He has to look at his mother's attitude toward him as reflecting her attitude toward herself and her own life lesson to learn to stand up for herself. Separate yourself from your parents' problems, don't let them control your life, and don't use them as excuses. You have a choice!

Our parents' self-regard has a determining influence on how they treat us. That is why it is important to understand that if they didn't give us as much love as we would have wanted, they actually didn't give enough to themselves either. If they didn't respect themselves, they couldn't respect us either. That's why it is a waste of time for us to still want this from them and to blame them, until they are ready to deal with it themselves. Some people are able to reach certain goals in their lives only once their parents have died. If our parents don't believe that we can achieve something, we have a constant problem in their eyes, because we, in a way, take on their attitude toward us, and we don't defend ourselves even though things work fine with other people.

Sometimes, however, parents behave toward their children in just the opposite way. They give them constant attention and care, and they call it love. Let's not confuse love with control and dependence. Many parents control their children through this overparenting and by making the children's goals more important than their own. In this way, they create in their children feelings of guilt about the love that their parents are overgiving them, and consequently, the children have a feeling that they are indebted to their parents. It is important that we should understand that children are not our property, despite the fact that in most languages, we say, "I have a baby!" They are living with us for a while, and our task is to teach them the things we know best—with our own lives, simply by what we do ourselves. We can teach them to be careful, but not to be fearful; we can teach them independence and respect, but not dependence.

Children learn the most from the relationship between their parents. They create models and expectations in this way for their later relationships with partners. We can tell what kind of models the parents were to their children first of all by what kind of partner they later choose. One time, a twenty-two-year-old woman came to me and complained that she was now dating her third boyfriend and that each of her boyfriends has been a truck driver. They were on the road a lot, and she didn't like that. She didn't understand it, but she had the feeling that other guys don't really even exist. She suspected that she was causing this herself. During the unblocking session, we dealt with situations in her childhood when she was at home alone all the time with her mother, and her father was constantly away. He was always traveling, and the girl's mother would cry a lot. The girl learned to blame her father for not taking care of them; in this way, she was able to participate in her mother's energy. That with which we overidentify, we become ourselves as well, and we will experience similar situations in our own life. She learned from her parents that a partner equals someone who is never home, and this model was expressed in her own choice of partners, because she chose those people who had the potential to provide her with what her father gave her mother—not being home.

What is this young lady supposed to learn from her parents? Perhaps how to stand up for a full-fledged-partner relationship, where both partners are present, and if a partner prefers to be on the road and prefers life outside the family, to accept this and to simply choose someone else.

Extreme blocks for future relationships arise in the case of superior and subordinate relationships between parents. In these situations, it can happen that in order to avoid getting into a similar situation as our parents, we prefer to avoid relationships altogether. If, for example, our father drank a lot and beat our mother and we had to watch this all through our childhood, most of the time, we will blame our father who was tyrannizing Mother. It rarely occurs to us that our mother was an even bigger problem because she allowed it all to happen, and with her attitude, she taught us subordination and an incapacity to stand up for ourselves. In this case, it is better to avoid relationships, because we are missing the model of a person who values themselves. And we know that we would bring Mother's powerlessness against Father into our partner relationships.

Our parents influence us even if we don't consciously know their attitudes and choices. It can even happen that in certain life situations, we behave according to their model at exactly the same age as they did. Let me tell you a story of a young lady, which fascinated me.

The young lady was very pleasant, nice, and pretty, but she was hopeless and full of tears. She was supposed to get married in two weeks, but she had just met a guy who enchanted her and offered her something that she couldn't expect to get from her future husband. She loved nature and the mountains and was always going on trips and weekend excursions, and her fiancé was not understanding about that at all. He wanted to be at home, and he bore a grudge against her about the mountains. He didn't want to travel anywhere, but he also didn't want her traveling either. The young man she had just met loved the mountains; excursions and trips really fulfilled him. And all at once, everything that she had willingly given up walked through the door. She knew that there was a person who offered what she was looking for. And what now? The wedding was prepared, dress made, parents waiting in joyous expectation. She was very unhappy about this and couldn't decide. Together we looked into what this was all about. The young woman "remembered" her mother's wedding day, in which she clearly saw that the person she was going to marry wasn't the person whom she wants as her partner. But she married him in spite of it. What can you do, right? It is the story of thousands of married couples—an accident. Could it be in our young lady's case an attempt to overcome her mother's block? If, in our deeply embedded intentions, we have this plan, we can pull into our lives a person who will help us with this task. So, my dear, what will you do? Will you behave as your mother did, or will you try something different? She was great; she tried something different. It is so important to want more out of life. She started to live with her new boyfriend, and they went on trips together. I love people's stories, and most of all, the stories of those who aren't afraid to try something new, and even more, those with happy endings, but most of all, those in which the people aren't afraid to stay true to themselves. Good luck, and love yourself . . .

Sometimes you see the opposite problem with parents—an overblown respect, children who make the parents godlike. I met a woman who lived alone, that is, with her parents, who were older, and she maintained that she could never find a partner who would be as perfect as her father. Some parents have a tendency to build in their children a feeling of their irreplaceability, and this takes away the children's power. Her father most likely wasn't actually all that perfect—because he didn't teach his little girl to have a healthy relationship with herself and to have self-confidence so that she will be able find a partner for herself, one who will fit her own images of a partner. Sons can also have the same opinion about their mothers—that no one takes care of them quite as well. By serving their sons, they make them dependent on their mothers. Sometimes it happens when a son lives alone with his mother that she gives up her own life and raises her son up to the level of a partner. Sometimes the son will join forces with the mother against the father. This creates a different combination, but in each case, any imbalance in our parents' relationship is expressed in our lives. Everything is expressed, absolutely everything. And we can always find the answer—the source of our problem—when we don't like something in our lives or when something goes wrong. Don't try to change your parents—just be yourself. Respect their path, but choose your own path, because the more problematic your relationship with your parents was, the more problematic your relationship with yourself is.

Parents are our roots—which we can't just tear out—we have to accept them. But what about the gypsy children abandoned by their parents and adopted by white parents? Rejection by one's own parents is usually expressed as low self-esteem, even in the case when the child gets everything it needs. But we have a choice!

Our parents are a source of great possibilities for us, but they are also a source of great limitations, which we will have to face and to deal with in our lives. But it is always to our advantage to accept our parents as they are, or as they were, and to believe that every second of their lives they behaved in the best way they knew how, even if we didn't like it at all—because now we have a chance to do it differently!

We are the source of our own success; let's understand what we were supposed to learn from our parents, and we can move on.

Chapter 12

_____ ⌒⌒ _____

Look at How Your Teachers Are Living

When we want to achieve certain goals in our lives, often the first thing we do is to look for instructions and guides on our path toward our longed-for skills. There isn't always something like that available, and so we search on. Of course, a lot depends on what we are trying to do. If, for example, we want instructions on how to use a computer, we can easily find something like that and get the information we need. If, however, we have a block against that activity (for example, if we don't believe we will be able to learn to use a computer), then we can attend a class, which we can probably find when we need it. But even then, it won't necessarily work out, and so we begin to call teachers into our lives. Most of the time, we need teachers when we don't have enough energy to reach a certain level or certain skills, and we need the energy of the teacher to support us on our path and to show us that the way is free and reachable. They take us through the first steps and support us in the activity and help us to see the first successes. But some activities, abilities, and skills can't be learned other than with the help of a teacher. We need feedback, and we need to be led.

For us, a teacher is someone who has a good command of a certain skill, ability, life attitude, or something that interests us and attracts us, and we want to learn this from this person. From that point of view, even five-year-old children can be teachers for us, with their capability to live in the present—and it would be very useful for us (at least sometimes) to accept a child as our teacher if we want to learn to live in the here and now. Even our dog can be a teacher for us. They will teach us to stand behind our decisions, because until we mean our commands to them seriously, they won't listen. Our children are our teachers because they teach us to know ourselves and to designate our boundaries.

Now let's focus on the teachers whom we consciously choose to bring into our lives and from whom we consciously want to be taught something that interests us very much, and we desire to learn their skill from them.

Imagine that on your spiritual journey you meet a person who seems very interesting to you. Maybe he has a self-confident look, noble features, long hair, and looks like a "real spiritual teacher," exactly how you would picture one. And maybe he says, "I am a teacher of relationships. Come with me, and I will teach you how to be happy in your relationships." Considering the mess you currently have in your life, and with relationships most of all, it is a tempting offer. Perhaps your inner self speaks, and you will want to ask him, "Master, how are your relationships in your life?"

"Me?" he answers. "I live alone in a cave in the woods. I don't have any relationships, I have solved those problems already. I don't need relationships anymore." Maybe you think that's a little weird. You have a different idea about what it means to be happy in your relationships. Maybe you would like to have a lot of friends, a good relationship with your partner, and joy in your communication with others. *But, okay,* you say to yourself, *he is a relationship teacher, and I really need that right now, so let's give it a try.*

What's going on here? Any teacher can only teach us what they themselves know. If your goal isn't to solve your relationship problems by you yourself going to live alone in a cave, this teacher doesn't have anything to teach you (that is, about relationships, but if you want to learn how to take care of yourself in the woods, that's another matter).

No one can truly teach you something that they don't live themselves! So look into the lives of your teachers!

Before you decide to become someone's student, look at how things are working in their life. See if they are truly **living what they say.** If you were going to learn Spanish, it would be a good idea to learn from someone who really knows it very well. This is clear. It would be more suspicious, for example, to meet an architect who is designing a home and interiors for you, and you find out while visiting his home that he actually lives with his family in one room at his parents' house. You don't see any sign of architectural ideas anywhere; everything is messy. And this is the person who is supposed to explain to you what is nice or interesting or what he has found that works in his professional career . . .

Even more problematic is a stockbroker, whom you are supposed to trust your money to in order to increase its value, who is poor as a church mouse and who is incapable of taking care of his own financial situation. You can guess how it will turn out with the money you give him. Less problematic is perhaps a very capable bricklayer who comes from a poor family and doesn't believe in attaining his own wealth. He will work his whole life on other people's houses and never have his own house. Most probably, however, there is nothing preventing him from building you a wonderful home, so he can be your teacher in home building. But he can't be your teacher in, for example, how to have your own home. As far as spiritual paths go, which we want to pass on other people, we can hardly pass on other people experiences that we have not gone through ourselves. We can never give to other people what we cannot give to ourselves. No one can teach you more than they themselves know. Look into the lives of your spiritual teachers to see if they really practice what they preach and if they really have a good command of what you want to learn from them.

Chapter 13

I Can't Assert Myself

"I can't assert myself, they are greedy, they will not let me." We often use this as an excuse why we couldn't achieve something we wanted, or why we didn't even try, because we knew ahead of time that it wouldn't work out. They are the reason we didn't do it—because they prevented us. "I can't fight," some people say. "I was raised by my parents to behave correctly, and because of that, I have nothing." They're implying that those people who did get what they want are probably getting it in a very indecent way and at others' expense. This is the way that many people present their lack of success and justify their inability to reach their goals. They create an intention for their lives, and they pull people into it, who want to walk all over them. We are endlessly creative and we create our reality according to our expectations. What we wish for, we get.

"By the time I am ready to speak, the others have been gone for a long time," realized a wonderful woman who now understands that the problem with her assertiveness isn't in other people but in her own hesitancy. She told me how it always takes her a long time before she is ready to talk, and by the time she opens her mouth, others are already talking about something else. She could probably still save the situation by interrupting the flow of conversation and letting them know that she would like to add something about the previous theme. But because she feels "weird" about it, later she feels even weirder. Then she can't concentrate, her debts pile up, and her participation in that specific community stops bringing her and the others anything.

Anytime we are participating in any life situation, we are not there by accident, of course. That is why it is important that we express ourselves and be who we are, in other words, to play our role, because it is by doing this that we keep events moving along. I remember once I visited a meeting of representatives of different schools of alternative education. The problematics interested me very much, but my alternative (the One-Brain method, which I was there representing) was too abstract even for some of the enlightened pedagogues, and so I ended up in more the role of the observer. Of course, this was due to my own doubts and to not being used to acting in this kind of arena. At one point, there was a great debate among the representatives about when the break would be and how long it would be. Most of these people knew one another already, and some took the opportunity to address old injuries and maybe to enhance their own importance, or perhaps unimportance. I didn't understand it, but I felt intensively that this was my moment. With just a few phrases, I would be able to stop the unpleasant situation and to name everything that was happening in that moment. But—I felt weird about jumping into it. I wanted to explain to them that we have a common goal and that the fighting is pointless, to really name the situation according to my experience and expertise. I hesitated, and therefore I missed the right moment. All of a sudden, from two seats over to the left, a young man who looked like he wasn't really participating in the momentary activity because he was caught up in his notebook turned toward me and said, "Lady, come on, say something finally. You know you understand it all!" Wham! That was information. That man must have just reacted completely intuitively on the basis of the energy I was sending. He received and reacted. He had caught me in the very act, and I really knew it . . . It is so important to express ourselves at the right moment because it is in our interest as well as in the interests of the others who need our feedback. Our excuses that others don't give us enough space don't solve anything because we are not going to feel any better—this is just an attempt to get back the energy we lost with our doubts about expressing ourselves.

If we have any kind of problem with the outside world, we have a problem with our self-confidence because we doubt our ability to take care of ourselves in a given situation. If we are decided and act in accord with the meaning of our lives, then the Universe comes to meet us, and we always get what we want. When we stand up for ourselves and take responsibility, others will usually satisfy us and give us what we ask for.

I really like spending time with children and making up various activities with them. I teach them to take responsibility for themselves, for what they feel, for their relationships, for their outcomes in various activities, and for their ability (or inability) to reach their goals. I want them to express themselves, and I respect them. There are big differences among the children as far as self-confidence goes, and I like to show them the advantages that come from believing in themselves. Let's say that one girl comes to ask me if she can go down to the creek. It doesn't happen often that kids go down there alone, but it's not unheard of. I look at the situation; I ask her, for example, if she can guarantee me that everything will be all right, if she won't fall, and if she can be back in fifteen minutes. If she looks at me with a blank look in her eyes, as if she doesn't understand me, I am most probably not going to let her go. If another girl came and answered the same question by eagerly agreeing with me and putting me at ease that everything will definitely be fine, then I will gladly let her go to the creek.

My daughter sometimes teaches children to ride horses, and she has similar experiences as well. She knows from experience that some children, in their desire to ride, start by saying, "I am definitely going to fall." It isn't much fun to work with children who have this plan, so my daughter negotiates a change in their program ahead of time. If there are other children there who don't plan to fall, she would probably give preference to them.

These are the results of the doubts, which we all feel in various situations. Sometimes we think that other people are refusing our request, but in reality, we are refusing it ourselves by our doubts. Other people, in this case, function as a mirror and confirm our doubts.

People feel better with people who are self-confident in their decisions. They don't give others any space for speculation because they have well-defined boundaries as well as well-defined ideas about what they want. They know that what they are currently doing is all right, and that is why they make choices easier for others, because they don't allow others to get in their way.

A beautiful story occurs to me in this context, which many of you know from Tolkien's *Lord of the Rings*. There, all the stories are about the significant roles of each of the participants, because everyone plays the right role at the right place in the right time. I remember when Frodo decided that he would separate from the group and go on with the ring himself. He knew for sure that was the right thing to do, and **so he did it**. In the same way that Sam was just as sure that his place was by Frodo's side—and that is why Frodo took him on. It was a wonderful moment when the group got to the place where Frodo went off by himself and some of them wanted to go with him. Only Aragorn was certain that Frodo should go on alone and that that was the way it should be. I don't mean that Aragorn was so clever and knew what was best for Frodo, but it was that he fully respected his assured decision and therefore knew that it was not his place. Thanks to this, he was able to see his own path more clearly and to do what was best for him . . . And that is how it is in all our lives.

If we know that this is our space, no one will interfere, because consciously or subconsciously, everyone wants to find themselves and to find their own space—special, perfect, and unique for each one of us.

Chapter 14

Chapter 14

Fear of Success

Many of us long for success and imagine it in the most colorful and wonderful dreams. Others react to the word *success* as if they have broken out in hives and behave as if it were something perfectly disgusting and wicked to talk about one's own success. Why? Why do we observe in people around us such varied reactions to success?

Perhaps it works like this: Each of us has lived through our childhood. Each of us has gone through various types of schooling. Most of the time, there was only one point to everything: achieving success. We all grew up in endlessly competitive environments where the best were also the most successful. To be successful most of the time meant simply to be better than others, to be ahead of them, to excel. Depending on how we handled this position, we created different attitudes to success. For example, perhaps we pretended that it didn't bother us that we weren't as successful as others because we were good at something else, even if we didn't know what that is. Sometimes the current competitive activity "didn't interest" us—because that was the way to be able to excuse our failure. If we weren't able to win at anything for a long while, we become masters of excuses of all kinds. To this day, some teachers who teach using so-called alternative educational methods still use a lot of competition in their teaching and maintain that children enjoy it. I know from experience that the children who win regularly enjoy these methods the most and that the rest are just passive or are enduring it in silence. On the other hand, those that win all the time begin to have problems with the fact that they are winning. If we earn our success through competition, then our success depends on the failure of someone else, and that corrupts our joy a little.

I remember while reading the aforementioned book *Mutant Message Down Under* being fascinated by the aborigines' attitudes toward competition. They don't understand the term because they support the goal of every individual, and each person in the society has a unique and indispensable place, which is not interchangeable with anyone else's. They are accustomed to making one another happy and, first of all, to making themselves happy. Dr. Morgan was excited by the way that the aborigines amuse themselves because they experience real joy. The aborigines were surprised at this attention and wanted to know how the "mutants," as they call us, amuse themselves. Mrs. Morgan thought for a while and then explained that one of their favorite games is competition. They didn't understand, so she explained. For example, two competitors step on a line, someone claps, and they run. The others stand on the sides and encourage them. Then the run is over—one of them is faster—and that one is the winner. Everyone is excited and claps a lot. The natives didn't understand. What else? Is that it? What do the people get their joy from? And what about the one who lost? What kind of fun is this when one is happy and the other is sad? We don't understand.

There is another equally important issue that comes out of this, because if our children are angry or sad when they don't come in first, we explain to them that then they should be excited that their friend won. If they don't get it, we begin to tell them that they don't know how to lose . . . But what is really going on here in the meantime with our success?

We have problems when we don't succeed, but we have problems even when we do succeed. How do we get out of this?

To simplify the whole situation, it is important to define what we have allocated in our minds to the concept of success. From all these lived experiences, some people's definitions are really interesting.

In most cases, however, these definitions aren't attractive enough in order for us to really want to achieve success. I will mention some definitions from my own practice, which are not very complimentary, though they are not very unusual . . . Some people see success as Overwhelming Others, Taking Advantage of Others, to Always Be the Best, to Never Make a Mistake, to Have No Friends, to Do Everything Yourself, to Have the Envy of Others, and so on. So you shouldn't be surprised anymore that even though people say they long for success, they in fact reject it internally because who would want it? What is your definition of *success* like, if success is constantly avoiding you?

Recently, a wonderful photographer came to me, wanting, at long last, success—so that everything in his life would work according to how he imagined it. But still he couldn't reach what he longed for. Photographers are free-thinking souls who like to be unobstructed, but the definition of the term *success* as this man saw it was this: a loss of freedom. And the result? No success, my friends. "No way, I can't do that for my success, because my freedom is the most precious thing I have If I am successful, I will have to work all the time and to dance to their music." But all that he had to do was to change the definition; that means to comprehend that even as a successful person he can be free and take responsibility for his success. And perhaps we had to look a bit into the past as well, to see what was happening there.

Some people have problems when in their lives the thing that they have long been calling for and desiring finally arrives. The thought they most often have is this: What if I lose it again? What if it doesn't work out? And in this ingenious way, we avoid the success, which is coming to us because we already "know" how it will turn out again.

I will tell you a very interesting story about a certain businessman. Later we laughed about this a lot, even though at the time it didn't seem funny to him at all. He had a special problem. Every time he was about to close on a specific order, when everything that had been in play was about to be put into action, and it was something he was going to profit from, he always felt suspiciously bad. And it got worse and worse, and he didn't understand why. The closer he was to success, the worse he felt. During unblocking his problem, we went back to a time when he was seventeen years old and had decided to go out with two friends to some dance parties. They were driving in his friend's father's car, which they had taken without asking because they didn't have driver's licenses. Silently, they pushed Father's car out of the garage and got on their way. Everything was going great. They went to one dance party, then to another, and had a whole night of going from club to club. They were satisfied, everything had gone off without a hitch, the car was fine, and they had a great time. They returned home toward morning, joyous at everything they had experienced and done. But as luck would have it, while putting the car back in the garage just before the successful end of their night of revelry, they crashed the car into the garage gate. The father woke up and flew off the handle.

If you have a feeling that there is something wrong also with your success, you can find your story, because

we are all as successful as we let ourselves be.

Chapter 15

_◦᠎᠎◦_

Poverty Isn't a Virtue—It's a Sickness

How many negative opinions and attitudes has each of us heard in our lives about the ability to make money and attain success? How many people have tried to make their poverty a positive quality, even a virtue? In reality, this is just a defensive position, because everyone yearns for a meaningful life free from want and full of opportunities to take full advantage of their potential. The majority of us yearn for a life free from fear about the days to come. We yearn for the opportunity to do what we want without worry and anxiety about how we're going to support ourselves. But most people don't believe they can achieve that, or they claim they do believe it's possible but that reality is somehow stagnant.

In truth, this is just another ingenious way not to go after your goal and not to be yourself. "I'd love to have this and that, but how am I supposed to come up with the money?" people often say. Or "I'd definitely go into business if I had at least a million" or even "If I had some money, man, I would live it up!" No, my friends, you wouldn't! It works in exactly the opposite way—because when you have a clear plan and a dream and you get rid of your negative systems of convictions regarding wealth and money, then you will be able to achieve your goals even if you don't have money. You'll simply find the money you need. But . . .

Once, an amazing woman came into my consultation room. She had decided when she was thirty-five years old that she was going to take her life into her own hands, to stop being dependent on her husband, and to start working on her own wealth and independence. She claimed that she was firm in her decision, but things still weren't working out how she wanted them to. She came from a poor background, so her mind was filled with limitations in the form of negative patterns regarding wealth. We discovered something interesting. During her consultation, we spoke about her fingernails a number of times. She had a problem with them—they kept breaking. I explained to her that our fingernails symbolize our aggressivity, that is, our ability to take care of, assert, and express ourselves. People who bite their nails, for example, are eliminating their ability to express themselves, usually because they think that nobody would be interested. When children do it, then it usually indicates the experience of a strict parenting style. By biting their nails, the children are both symbolically and actually getting rid of their own power because they're not able to defy their parents. But let's return to our young lady. She recalled a story from when she was five years old, or maybe a little older. She had been spending time with her grandmother, whom she loved very much. Her grandmother was telling some stories about her childhood, how because they were very poor they never had anything that they needed. The little girl listened attentively and then explained to her grandmother how she was going to do things when she grew up. She talked about all the wonderful things she was going to have. Her grandmother was appalled and promptly posed her granddaughter a very fundamental question: "Do you know why you have fingernails?" She stretched out the little girl's arm and said, "Whenever you reach for something you want, remember your fingernails. They'll say to you, 'Hands off!'" Good advice is worth its weight in gold! And so the little girl incorporated this advice into her life. Everything went smoothly—as long as the girl didn't want anything.

We integrate an endless supply of similar well-intentioned advice into our lives, and in most cases, we aren't even aware of it. For me, personally, it is wonderful news that we can figure it out and get rid of these limitations—if we really want to. Some people consider these limitations to be normal, and on top of that, they pass them on to their children, their friends, to everybody.

Sometimes we consciously pass on our blocks regarding wealth to our kids, because if we don't believe we can attain wealth, then we don't believe others can attain it either. We see it as our responsibility to explain "reality" to them. In this way, we "create" these limitations on our children's entire lives, which they then struggle with. And some of them, those who have accepted these limitations and allowed them to dictate their lives, don't even bother to struggle. Some of these limitations concern our basic needs, which we are consequently unable to provide for ourselves. Other limitations prevent us from realizing our dreams.

I'll tell you the story of an Austrian businessman who longed for a certain red Porsche, a vintage car he wanted to restore. He started working on his plan, but problems with the car kept popping up from the very beginning. Nothing was going according to plan—parts, time, money—there was always some problem. Some of the things he had to do even seemed pointless and quite tedious. He was extremely suspicious about why nothing was working out. We started looking for his problem. While unblocking him, we returned to when he was eight years old, when his family was celebrating Christmas. It was Christmas Eve, and gifts were being handed out. The boy got one particularly interesting gift, a box, which, when opened, revealed a beautiful red Porsche. He was elated. It was magnificent! A flood of thoughts started racing through his head, but his father abruptly set things right. "You'll never in your life have that kind of a car," he clarified, just in case the boy had been thinking he could. And what happened to the boy? Did he believe his father? Or did he not? We will see . . .

We are systematically brought up for "frugality," poverty, to so-called modesty. In most cases, this means that we stop believing that we can achieve what we want in life. Even as kids, we're very often criticized for wanting things. How often have you been witness to a debate between a mother and a son, the latter pointing to a Mercedes driving by, his eyes goggling out of his head? "That's such a cool car. I'm going to buy one of those when I grow up!" His mother is appalled, maybe even sad. If the goals of our children seem too grand for us, we often consider it our duty to "plant their feet back down on the ground." "That kind of car is too expensive," his mother responds. "You probably won't ever have enough money to buy it." All of which is usually followed by a heap of prudent advice. For example, how there are lots of much better cars, and even a lot cheaper. It all boils down to the fact that wanting that kind of a car is just plain dumb.

But the thing is, everything we see around us started as just an idea—maybe as just the dream of a little boy. Don't take kids' dreams away from them; teach them how to materialize them. Young children don't need to know how they're going to achieve their dreams yet, because for the moment, they're just putting ideas together about everything that is possible here on Earth. Teach them that they are the rulers of their lives and that they have the ability to create everything they want; they just have to learn to respect certain rules.

The thing is that we primarily teach them by the example of our own life. We can't teach our children or anybody else how to be wealthy if we are poor. We can't achieve our own goals if we spend all our energy on supporting ourselves, or in some cases, just surviving. Having all we need in life to develop and live a full life is part of basic self-respect. The goal probably isn't wealth in and of itself, but the ability to create the kind of wealth that serves us on our life path toward maximal self-expression.

Get rid of your negative attitudes toward wealth. There is enough here for everyone. The source is endless, and it depends entirely on you which path you choose. We can always attain everything we need in our lives as long as we truly believe we can. And when will we know that we truly believe? Well, once we attain what we want, of course . . .

Let's spend a little more time thinking about the money issue. It's an important subject we are dealing with all the time. People who are most interested in money are the ones who don't have it. Some even create the conviction that money is filthy and evil—but they are lacking money all the time. Others claim that money isn't the least bit important: "I don't need money for anything." Many people purport to be "spiritual" and disdain money. I recall talking with one young man about my work, and he was very interested in my workshops. He said he'd very much like to take part, but he immediately complained that they were expensive and that he couldn't afford them. I asked him how much he made, and he replied about six thousand crowns a month.[5] I was quite astonished, but he didn't even let me articulate my surprise. "It's not like I don't have anything, and what I do have is enough. You know, money isn't important to me. I'm all right," he assured. It didn't make sense to me. "So you would like to participate in my workshop?" He sighed slightly and nodded . . . Stop playing this hypocritical game with yourself, because if you don't have enough money for something, then you don't have enough, and you need to deal with that. The first step is admitting that if you want something, it's completely all right and it's also completely all right that you want money for it. So the goal isn't money, but money's the way you can realize your plans. And if our goals—and therefore, we—are important, then so is money because "You can't foot the bill when you're flat broke."

In order to make financial progress, we need to accept that money is a part of our life, because insofar as we were born into an era where the expression of our social worth is through money, then it's important to stop going against that grain because it's unlikely any of us will be able to influence it. Not long ago, a man came to consult me. After asking him what he wanted to resolve, he became angry and barked, "I'm out of fucking money again." He assumed that if money didn't exist, he wouldn't have his life problem . . . But that's not the way things work. The fact is that money exists, and the only way to stop worrying about money is to have it. By having a positive attitude toward it, we attract it and money-magnetize ourselves, because money is an energy that's constantly flowing. My ten-year-old son is an important source of enlightenment for me.

---

5   Translator's note: Six thousand crowns is about one-third the average Czech salary, analogous to something like $12,000 a year in the United States.

Once, he asked me for fifty crowns for just a "silly little thing," which I thought was a waste of money, so I didn't give him any. Within the next couple of hours, he had found a fifty-crown bill at the bus stop— exactly the amount he needed. He became so fond of this pastime that he found two more fifty-crown bills that day, one of which he found during a walk in the woods with me. I found the whole thing completely unbelievable. The bill was just lying on the forest path, all crumpled up and dirty, just waiting for him . . . I wouldn't even have noticed it myself, but the truth is, I wasn't looking.

Of course, that doesn't mean that we'll just find everything we're looking for. There are thousands of ways to attract what we need, as long as our energy is unequivocal and free of conflict. Sometimes it's interesting to ask ourselves, "Why is it still 'profitable' for me not to have money? What sort of an illusion of myself am I maintaining? What do I keep avoiding?" Playing things honestly is sometimes very difficult, because not having money is socially acceptable sometimes, and many people think it's normal. But we can change that by admitting that it no longer works for us and that we will continue searching our subconsciousness for the limitations that we've created in our lives, and we will change our programming . . .

because poverty isn't a virtue, it's a sickness!

Chapter 16

Ask and You Will Receive

Often at my lectures I tell a certain story. Most of the time, I start off by saying that I am going to tell a joke, but today I am not so sure anymore that it's a joke. In any case, I think that this is exactly the way that things work. It is about all the people who don't give themselves what they long for, who don't see the opportunities, who put off what they want in their lives—and what's worse, it doesn't even occur to them that it could be okay to want it. This is a very common event here on Earth, and it appears in endless forms and on endless levels.

So here it is: Once upon a time, there lived a man who died. He got to heaven and met Saint Peter, who led him to a beautiful home and said to him, "You're going to live here. This is your new home. Take a look around." Looking at his new home, the man was very surprised. It was perfect, exactly what he would have wished for in his most secret dreams. As he walked from room to room, he couldn't get enough of the splendor and variety of the furnishings and ingenious equipment, which he so appreciated and admired. His whole life he had always enjoyed improving things, inventing various gadgets to make life around the house more convenient. Unfortunately, during his life, he didn't always have time to do this, so he just bought whatever happened to be on the market at the time. Of course, for the rest of his life, he would curse those things for being badly designed. Now he really felt like he was in paradise. There was just one thing that wasn't right. All the rooms in the house were full of some kind of strange boxes. They were everywhere. They were boxes of different sizes, from large to small. There were some huge ones, but many were rather small too. He shook his head and asked Saint Peter, "Why are there so many boxes everywhere?" Saint Peter thought for a moment and said, "Well, have a look for yourself. Just go closer, and you will understand." The man went up to look at the first package and saw something strange—his name and address were written on it. He looked at some other boxes, and they had his name and address on them too. His name was everywhere. He still didn't understand and asked Saint Peter, "I don't get it. My name is on all of them. And you see over here, on all of them there is this stamp Return to Sender." Saint Peter laughed and said, "You still don't understand? Those are all undelivered presents, your unfulfilled wishes, which you ordered but didn't pick up. They were undeliverable. Either you forgot that you wanted them, or you thought that you would never get them. They were returned to us, and we saved them for you. Here is everything you ever wished for. So enjoy." Saint Peter slowly disappeared. The man sat there and began to unpack his things. Absolutely everything was there—from rainbow-colored balls he wanted as a kid to a hobby horse with a real tail, to the beautiful necklace he had longed to give his wife. He unwrapped things as if in a dream, and his whole life ran before his eyes . . . He wondered, thoughtfully, how many of the things that he wanted then did he actually give to himself? But the rooms were so full that he just unwrapped and unwrapped . . . and unwrapped. And our story ends here, but this man may be unwrapping still.

So did you like it? So you see, you don't have to fear; you will get everything in the end. They will save everything for you, and you will have it upstairs—if that is enough for you.

So how many of your wishes (of those which you are aware of) were you able to fulfill without making excuses, like it wasn't realistic, that it's not the right time, that it just wasn't possible, or in the end that you decided "rationally and realistically," that you don't even really want it?

I love Bärbel Mohr's book *The Cosmic Ordering Service* and the other books in her series, where she explains how it all works, or doesn't work, as the case may be. I really like her open and real way of expressing herself and her explicit information about how, in our lives, everything develops on the basis of our own intentions. If we realize this, then we can create our lives the way we imagine them. So you can begin ordering.

The Universe is prepared to fulfill your every wish, but if you have the feeling that you perhaps don't deserve it or that it would disturb the neighbors or if it is not a humble wish (whichever applies to you), as you already know, they will keep it for you upstairs . . .

Get to know your own mechanism—with whose help you can gradually get what you want. Start ordering. Trust the Universe, but at the same time you should, over time, get rid of your own limitations, by which you are destroying the fulfillment of your wishes. First learn to observe how things happen and then find the feeling you have during these times—because you are the creator. Maybe it's best to start with observing a small fulfilled wish, something that isn't even so important for you, and so you didn't even bother to take subversive measures that would impede the universal laws in their attraction and endless creativity from acting on your request.

I imagine it something like this: One day not too long ago, our whole family was at home; each of us was spending time on our own activities. The sun was shining bright, and it revealed different hidden corners of our house, and we were suddenly seized by a desire to clean up. Our house had lacked a proper broom for some time, but it wasn't such a huge problem that anybody was willing to deal with. While my boyfriend, Peter, was sweeping in the downstairs hall, he kept mumbling under his breath at our horrible broom. "We have to get a new one," he said, and at the same time he clearly sent out the thought that he definitely wasn't going out to buy it right now. A few hours later, there was a ring at the front gate. Peter opened the door and saw a woman he didn't know who was selling wonderful new handmade brooms, which were sold for half the price that they would normally cost in the store. She smiled in a strange way, took the money, and went on her way . . . Simple, isn't it? Good work.

Everyone has similar stories. Start to collect them and notice the perfect synchronicity of individual intentions—because everything is perfect, unless you are inhibiting it. What kind of coincidence is this when you think of needing a new broom and the new broom is offered to you at the same moment? Someone rings the bell and has a look on her face that is saying, "So here is your broom . . ."

There is no such thing as a coincidence.

Don't be afraid to name it and to fully admit what you want. If you don't have clear intentions, any creation is impossible. I am talking about creation as creating what you want, because we are always creating. Of course, we can also use our creativity to make what we don't want; it is also creation, although sometimes it's very unpleasant. Sometimes we are trying so hard to manipulate reality so it will be exactly how we think that we ordered it—but it doesn't work because we simply haven't ordered it like that. If we don't get what we think we wanted, we have to figure out where the mistake was.

I'll tell you a story about a time when I tried to get more from a situation than I ordered, but it didn't work out.

Once, I was putting my things in order and having some fliers and informational brochures printed. It cost quite a bit of money, and I thought that that would be enough. But then I realized that I needed new business cards too. I was dissatisfied; I knew that I just wasn't willing to spend any more money to have them made right then. I was annoyed about it, but I decided just not to think about it. I was working on something else when my telephone rang. The woman on the phone line urgently wanted to see me. It had to be today; she had big problems. She was a little confused but determined. We agreed that she would come that day, in the evening. That evening, a very pleasant young woman with big worries came into my office and said, "Please, I really need to be unblocked, but I don't have any money to pay you—that is the problem I want to work on. But if you don't mind . . ." she was silent. I looked at her questioningly. "If you don't mind," she continued, "I can make you some business cards in exchange." That was something! We decided on the details, the number of unblocking sessions that would equal the worth of the business cards, and I had them in a few days. The young woman felt better and better, and her life began to change. But I had a great idea. "Maybe," I said to myself, "since that seems to work so well, I can get some other things too." So as the limit of the agreed unblocking sessions drew toward its conclusion, I wanted to make another deal. But for some reason, it was not working out.

It just wouldn't happen—the young lady kept putting it off again and again. She said that she probably wasn't going to work there much longer and so on. So I stopped pushing her because now I understood that my order had been the business cards and nothing more. I guess she was glad now because she knew her job was done. There was nothing more to do, so she didn't show up again. Thank you for the great business cards.

So sometimes it is very important to recognize whether the situation that we are currently in is really bringing what we asked for, or whether what we asked for is even contained in the relevant situation. Sometimes we are blinded by what we want, usually in some ideal form, and we don't see that that is not what the situation is bringing. Then we get fixed on this single possibility and have the tendency to manipulate reality. We just don't see some things, and we get into problems. This happens often in relationships, when, for example, we are looking intensively for a partner, and during the first meeting, we convince ourselves that this guy is **it**. Perhaps it's true that some little thing isn't quite right, for example, that he has lots of friends whom he spends a lot of time with at the bar, or that he is often broke, but we have a feeling that eventually that will go away. But most of the time, it doesn't go away. Those things that bothered us at the beginning, and which we in our noble-mindedness overlooked, grow larger and larger until eventually we have to deal with the situation anyway. It is important to accept that if our reality isn't **it**, then we have to correct the order and either leave the situation or accept it as a step along the way and, knowing what it is that we want, go on. Sometimes we can't achieve our goals all at once, but gradually. So we mustn't forget where we want to go.

Reach your goals *gradually*, but don't forget where you want to go.

Now I want to tell you one last story. This one is about my daughter, and it always fills me with great pleasure.

When she was young, she very early on expressed interest in various animals. Later this interest narrowed into dogs and horses. She collected different pictures of horses, and so I bought her encyclopedias of dogs and horses for her birthday. When she was a little older, she would often flip through those books before bedtime; her room was full of pictures of horses as well. Then there were bedcovers with pictures of horses—for several years, she never slept without them. I didn't pay too much attention to it, because as a young girl, I was crazy about horses too, and so it fit into my definition of "normal" for a girl of her age. I had horses classified under the heading of "unfulfillable dreams," and I obviously behaved as if it must be the same case with her. But still I bought her books and bedspreads and thought that would be the end of it. My daughter had another idea. She really wanted to have a dog. I didn't want to let her, and so I used the silly excuse that it would be better to wait until her brother was a little older so he would know how to treat a dog. Now I know that in reality, I did want a dog as well; my husband was the one who didn't want one. I didn't believe he would "allow" us to have the dog, so I put it off for another time. And then I made a requirement that if we have to get a dog, then it should be a dachshund because that was the dog my parents had, and so that was the only dog I would have myself. I thought the whole idea was on hold, until one day my daughter came home with a three-month-old dachshund, whom she said she had found at the station. Or had he found her? That dog stayed with us and, to this day, is an important member of our family. My daughter was ten years old then, and since that time, everything has gone smoothly. She started going to various horse-riding clubs—she didn't have it easy because she was small and because I didn't take her so seriously. But she was persistent even though she only got to be near horses every once in a while; although I think it actually included a lot of work with the wheelbarrow and prong. Then one day a young woman rang our bell and asked for my daughter, Michala. She said she heard that she is interested in horses and that she herself had just bought one. She offered my daughter that they could look after the filly together. The corral was just two minutes from our house. My daughter started to live her dream to ride. After a while, the same lady came again, with another offer, "I think we can fit two horses in that space, that way we could ride together." This time I took part, and I bought Michala a horse. She chose a Hucul filly, and from time to time, she took part in some races with her lady friend. For a long while they had great times together, racing trains and running around in the fields. They went grocery shopping and to the pub for a soda with the horses.

Maybe this all seems completely normal to you.

Okay then, so don't delay and place your orders!

Chapter 17

Our Children

Your children are not your children.
They are the sons and daughters of Life's longing for itself.
They come through you but not from you,
And though they are with you yet they belong not to you.
You may give them your love but not your thoughts,
For they have their own thoughts.
You may house their bodies but not their souls,
For their souls dwell in the house of tomorrow, which you
cannot visit, not even in your dreams.
You may strive to be like them, but seek not to make them
like you.
For life goes not backward nor tarries with yesterday.
You are the bows from which your children as living arrows
are sent forth.
The archer sees the mark upon the path of the infinite, and
He bends you with His might that His arrows may go swift
and far.
Let your bending in the archer's hand be for gladness;
For even as He loves the arrow that flies, so He loves also
the bow that is stable.

—Kahlil Gibran's *The Prophet*, from the chapter
"Children"

It may be that in every single language in the world we say, "I have a baby." We consider children to be our property. These forms of ownership are expressed in endless variations. It begins with completely innocent thoughts such as these: we would like our child to be what we wish them to be, what kind of knowledge and skills we want our child to have in its life, or we have ideas about where and how our child should live and what kind of partner would be best for our child to find. Perhaps a rich husband or a capable one, one who doesn't travel too much and who takes care of the family, if we have a girl. And what about some boys' mothers' expectations? Perhaps they are concerned that the daughter-in-law should take good care of their son, to know how to cook what he likes to eat, and be tidy (but not too tidy so she doesn't harass him too much, you know, he really isn't into cleaning). These small and not so small parental manipulations result in parents constantly stepping into their children's life paths, and very often (although it is done with the best of goodwill), they lead them away from their goal. The problem often lies in the fact that parents pass off their own attitudes and life truths hard-won on the basis of their experience as universal laws, and they often force this on their children as the only possible path. This can feed guilt feelings in children who don't follow their parents' path and make it impossible for them to freely create their own attitudes toward themselves and, consequently, toward others and the whole world. Thus, children, if they have ideas that are different from their parents', they feel guilt and separation for not having the same ideas as them, even if their parents' ideas are unacceptable to them. In the future they will have a problem with their difference, and they will have the impression that the world expects them to suppress their ideas. If they are different than others or have different views, then they will constantly have problems with it. So they become dependent mainly on the evaluations of other people, which is a general problem of almost all people. And all this because they have lost contact with their own selves. I would like to tell everybody **that our purpose and our goal are in the very fact that we are different, in our individual path that is unique and incomparable to anyone else's.** The world is made up of many points of view, from different paths and attitudes, which, even if we don't like them or they are unacceptable to us, they aren't standing against us as we often see it. The different attitudes of others simply complement our worldview. We become aware of more possibilities of how to see things. We can choose! In our own thoughts, we are free beings, and the more points of view on the world that we can put together, the more we understand the world. It is important to stand up for our opinions, but it is even more important to tell our children this:

This is how I do it. This is my truth and my path, but there are other truths and paths as well, of course.

If children knew that life is about finding one's own path and not fighting for one truth, that it is normal and even necessary that everyone should think differently and live different lives, then I think they wouldn't have to do so many stupid things that aren't good for them and that they often don't even want to do during puberty when children are trying to stand up for themselves. Because during that time, they have an endlessly powerful need simply to be **different** even at the price of being destructive to themselves and to anything around them that restricts them as they say. They want to defy; they want to assert themselves! Why do they have to use these sometimes-drastic ways of differentiating themselves and forcing adults to accept them? Because they don't know that being different is completely normal? Aren't they aware of their responsibility for their own path?

And what about those little blackmails and creating fears in children, which parents sometimes use in order to force children to do something that they can't defend in a normal way? I'll tell you a story I heard about a little girl.

The girl's name was Nora. She was wonderful and very clever. She was four years old. One day, though, she came home from school unbelievably dirty. Her mom got angry. "Well, that's not the kind of little girl we want around here at all. You'll have to find another home because we don't want any dirty slobs living around here," Mom said. Those were tough words. We could call this emotional blackmail, but Nora had her own explanation. She went to her room, where she had her little suitcase under the bed. She took it out and began to fill it up. She put all her teddy bears, a pillow, some clothes, and some coins from her piggybank in and shut the suitcase. She took a last look around her room, slid toward the front door, and shut the door behind her. It was already nighttime, and she walked down her street two blocks until she came to the police station. She knew the place because it was on the route that she and her mom used to walk to kindergarten. She went inside and rang the buzzer. The officer on duty looked at her, surprised. "Hello," said Nora. "My mom told me that I am supposed to look for a new home, that she doesn't want me, so I came here. Please help me to find it." The policeman wondered. "Hmm, so they don't want you, you say . . . okay, we'll have a look . . . and why don't they want you at home?" he asked. The little girl Nora explained everything to him. It didn't take long for the phone at Nora's parents' house to ring . . . You can imagine yourselves how that story ends. The parents had a great fright, and they both understood that they would never do that again. And their wonderful Nora? What a wonderful child; she didn't forget who she was, and she wasn't going to let herself be blackmailed. It was a perfect lesson for her parents.

Never threaten your children with something you aren't willing to do!

Not all children are like Nora. It isn't easy for children to stay themselves. It's almost impossible! Some are afraid and don't trust themselves and the world very much. They fear they will lose the people close to them, and so they are willing to do anything to prevent it. Children also become the subject of manipulation in relationships when parents try to solve their problems through the children—most of the time, the parents try to control each other exactly through their relationship with the children, or they try to get the children on their side. It isn't really surprising, though, because many children were conceived, thanks to pressure on one of the partners' sides, not from love and respect toward each other. Many children are blackmailed and taught to fear: to fear life, to fear want, to fear being alone, and to fear a life without love.

We teach them by how we deal with them how to value or not to value themselves, life, and all the values that can be sacred or completely profane and pointless.

I would like to quote from the end of one chapter of the book *Real Moments: Discover the Secret for True Happiness* by the author Barbara De Angelis. I love this book, and it speaks to my heart. I love her stories and her honest way of expressing herself. Thank you for the beautiful words; I couldn't have said it better myself.

Children are . . . ancient souls in tiny bodies. (*Master Adalfo*)

Your children are not your children. They are your teachers, guides, challengers, advice-bringers, truth-revealers, heart-healers, and soul-menders. They are in connection with the source of wisdom and love, which many of us, during our process of growing up and getting old, have lost. They see angels and practice unconditional love, and they know the cosmic connections.

All children are little mystics. They easily travel between the visible and invisible worlds. They haven't let themselves be caught yet in the borders of space and time. They know how to fly.

Until we hold them back with our ideas about what is real and what isn't real, all children hold within them a natural spirituality. **They remember things that we have forgotten; what's sad is that we force them to forget too when we don't respect their natural knowledge or we disallow it.**

I'll tell you a beautiful story that I heard a while ago from a mother whose second child had just been born, another boy. One evening when she came into the baby's room, she saw her firstborn, who was three years old at the time, standing next to his brother's crib, looking at the tiny body lying inside. She didn't want to disturb anything, so she stayed standing at the door. She saw her older son lean in toward the newborn and whisper in a conspiratorial tone,

"Shh! Hey . . . Jimmy. It's me . . . your brother, Danny. Tell me, what does God look like? I'm starting to forget."

Tears came to the eyes of the mother, who was witness to this blessed and real event. She realized that Danny knew that Jimmy had just come from the kingdom of Spirit, from the world that Danny still remembers in patches but is losing contact with because he was identifying more and more with his physical body and with his role as the male being Danny. He hoped in his secret discussion with Jimmy to refresh the truth, which he felt was every day sliding away from him into realms beyond return.

I like this story. It says everything we need to say about what our children actually are.

> **Welcome them into your life as your teachers and your blessings. Let them show you how to find and how to celebrate the meaning in every moment . . . And if you too have forgotten how God looks, ask your child to help you remember . . .**

Thank you, Barbara. Once again, thank you.

I would also like to thank my own children for all the lessons that they have given me. I remember with love all the wonderful moments when they were small and when their tiny hands began to take hold of the world. For their courage, joy, and excitement, for their trust and honesty, for the perfect acceptance I got from them.

They gave me so much love and so much hope. They helped me to remember my dreams at a time when I was slowly erasing them from my life. It was about time too, because I was already beginning to lose myself in my life. We played so much and were together so often that I had a perfect opportunity to learn how to take advantage of the present moment from masters. They had so many ideas and instantly began to realize them, because living wasn't a problem for them.

And that is why I support my children, and all children, to be themselves, to stay who they are so they can go on giving me and other people the wonderful news about us all, and to not be afraid to express themselves!

You will never learn so much about yourself from anyone other than your children. You will never be so important for anyone else. Don't manipulate your children, and let them express themselves! Then you will learn a lot about yourself!

Don't let your children run your life, but let them be themselves. Don't teach them to fear but to believe in themselves and in their own power.

Thank you to all children for our past, present, and future meetings.

Chapter 18

Sex Is an Expression of Your Self-Love

Sex is an expression of our self-love, when it works and also when it doesn't work. Through love of another person, we are in fact transferring love to ourselves. Through the attention of another person, we give attention to ourselves. Through physical contact with a loved person, we meet with ourselves. Or don't meet, as the case may be.

Once, a young man brought his wife with him into my consultation room. "Please unblock her," he said decidedly. I raised my eyebrows in question, and he explained, "She has a problem with sex."

"Hmm." I nodded, because it always amuses me how other people know exactly what another person's problem is. "And how is this expressed?" I asked. "Well, she just doesn't want to sleep with me at all. She has a problem, she has to solve it," he explained again intensely. "And you don't have a problem with sex?" I asked him. "No, I am fine, I could do it all the time," he explained urgently. "And why do you have a wife who doesn't want to sleep with you if you don't have any problem with sex?" I pushed a bit. He was silent. I think he understood.

The amount of love we get from our partners is simply and only just about us, because we choose our partners ourselves. On the basis of what? On the basis of our self-love, on the basis of what we want to give ourselves, on the basis of how we love ourselves, and also on the basis of our blocks from childhood, because most of the time, we fulfill the relationship model that we get from our parents.

Very few children live in an environment of their parents' love-filled relationship. Just a few children are witness to an accommodating understanding between their parents on both the mental and physical sides. When asked about their parents and sex, many people make amazed faces and are unable to imagine that their parents could be "doing it too."

Sex is an eternal theme in our lives. It is one of the most perfect means of staying in the present moment because sexual stimuli are very strong. If we are serious about it, then most of the time, we don't have space in our heads for other thoughts. Although it's true that some people can manage it. They just fake their excitement out of a lack of joy and spontaneity and, in this way, cheat themselves and their partners as well. We have been blocked toward sex for generations; our possible negative experiences from childhood add to the problems of generations. The church is responsible for many guilt feelings connected with sex; the church manipulated the populace, creating guilt feelings in connection with feeling of physical fulfillment, which was very often seen as a sin. Girls were stuck in passive roles, and many died in the bonfires in the time of witch hunts because of these connotations. Being beautiful, full of life, and fulfilled in their role as women in a joyful and creative way was considered sinful, and it created fear in some men. It was necessary to get rid of it. Men, who were focused on their left brain hemispheres— that is, fear, control, and fighting—feared the women, who excited and attracted them with their self-confidence, which they created on the basis of being connected with their right hemispheres, which represents creativity, joy, emotionality, and presence. And all this is present in sex as well. The time for equality between men and women is coming, the time for balance between the two hemispheres of the brain, the male and the female. The time for the fulfillment of both polarities, the time for love, honor, and equality is coming. It is time to stop playing the masculine and feminine roles created over the centuries. It's the end of the war of the sexes—it is time to be man or woman in fullness and full equality.

Sex is the highest form of creativity because a great deal of energy results from the interaction of men's and women's opposite polarities. Sex means the same thing for adults that caressing and physical contact with their parents do for children. That is why problems in adulthood always relate to fulfilled or unfulfilled contact in childhood. Some children do not know unconditional caressing and don't see their parents in an honest and loving embrace, and therefore they don't have a good model for sex. A clear and basic requirement for a functioning sexual relationship is, first of all, a partnership and an understanding on a spiritual level. By a partnership, I mean an equality of both partners in mutually respecting their goals and two-way support in reaching them. It means being helpful in solving shared issues, showing interest, and having open communication. By equality, I mean that the partners are able to agree on priorities without one of them suppressing themselves or the other partner. I consider a good partnership to be a condition of complete trust in the fact that **you are the best for me and I am the best for you**. Then the physical side of the relationship can work as well. Often people complain that their sex life doesn't work, but most of the time, we find that it is really the whole relationship that doesn't work. Sometimes possible problems seem to the partners to be normal, and so they don't try to solve them. But this usually comes out in sex. If, for example, there is a problem in the mutual respect between two partners, in their constant competition and humiliation of each other, then during sex, which is a perfect act of trust and respect, this model will show its teeth. Sometimes it even makes shared experience impossible. If we don't believe in the love of the other person, then we can't be fulfilled by physical contact with them. The result of this is the problem that our "sex life doesn't work." Thus, the expression of highest love becomes a purely physical act, which most of the time we don't enjoy and doesn't satisfy us. For many couples, sex then becomes a serious subject of manipulation, mutual blackmailing, and further humiliation.

What some people call a problem with sex is, in many cases, simply that we make love to the wrong person, at the wrong time, or for the wrong reasons.

Then we often don't want to express ourselves; we are waiting for the reaction from our partner, and they are waiting for ours. If we don't make love out of love, many problems come up. Spontaneity, playfulness, and trust disappear, and we lose energy after the sexual act instead of gaining it. The encounter with ourselves as well as with the other person doesn't come, and we feel rejected. Our own rejection...

Once, a twenty-year-old girl came into my consultation room complaining about her relationships with guys. She was just provoking them sexually, and she was never able to create a serious relationship. About herself she knew that she behaved as if she was superior, and it seemed that she had had enough of it. She told herself again and again that she wasn't going to do it, but then she would manipulate guys and demean them again and again. She didn't understand why she did it because it seemed to her that this wasn't bringing her any satisfaction.

In our present life, whenever we can't overcome our unsuitable model of behavior, there is always some experience from childhood that lies behind it, which we are still using even though it isn't working for us. We need to return to where we decided to behave in a certain way and to find a possibility to look at the situation a little differently. In this particular case, it was her **conception**. This is an important moment in our lives that directly determines our own value that we give to ourselves in our life. Our parents' way of behaving, intentions, and relationship at the time of conception will determine our starting conditions—because mostly, we pull all that into ourselves. This very much affects our future relationship to sex, among other things.

Every second of our lives is saved in our memories, and if we want to recall something, all of us always can. And now a story. The girl was recalling her parents at a particular time. Her parents were in bed. The mother was lying down, and the father was sitting up, looking at her. At first glance, it seemed as if Mother was sleeping. Father was indecisive and didn't know what to do. His indecision was downright palpable, and the energetic charge of the whole situation made the girl very uncomfortable. After she thought for a while, she understood that Mother wasn't sleeping at all. She was only pretending that she was sleeping, and Father was watching her helplessly. The whole situation was marked by manipulation by her mother, but with her father's consent, because two are needed for every manipulation. There is the one who does and the one who allows it. You can't have one without the other, and neither is worse or better than the other. Everything is like darkness and light . . .

I looked into which of the parents is really a problem for the girl. So most of the time, we lean toward one of the "guilty ones," and that is the source of our imbalance, because we aren't capable of seeing the whole situation in its mutual connections. Everything is like darkness and light—the one creates the other. The behavior of one promotes the behavior of the other one, and the result of this imbalance is that both are dissatisfied. "So how does the story continue? Does something happen?" I asked. The girl was really very disturbed by her mother, who doesn't express her feelings, and she wanted Father to express himself instead, or she just avoided contact with him in this primitive way. After a while, she found out that, in fact, her father irritates her even more than Mother with his passivity and not expressing what he wants—if he wants anything. So what should we do with this? Her conception. It happened something like that . . . What did she learn from that situation? What attitude toward sex did she choose for the future, and why did she choose it? The girl breathed in and screamed angrily, "Do something, or I am not going to be born!"

Stop manipulating! Express what you want and give others their choice to express themselves. Risk success; express what you want— if, of course, you know what you want. Most of the time you will get what you want! We put all the connections together with this girl. She understood why she brought guys into her life that would let her toy with them, and she decided to finish with it. Our parents give us lessons that sooner or later we have the potential to deal with. We are free in our lives, and we are also free to decide how we want to enjoy sex.

Perhaps, it will occur to you what people who were conceived through rape bring into their lives. What does their sex look like? And what about those whose mothers decided to entrap their fathers because they knew that they didn't want a baby? There are as many stories as there are people.

Value yourself and put your sexual life in order. Enjoy life joyously and freely. Enter the library of your subconsciousness, and you will meet with all the information you need. Love yourself, love your body, perceive your feelings . . . love life! And you will meet with the truth.

Chapter 19

_◌◌_

My Story

I'm not one of those people who make dramatic trips to Africa and experience some adventurous pilgrimage on the border of life and death. But looking back at my life, there were definitely situations from time to time when I saw my life in equally serious and dramatic terms—and I felt threatened, as if my life really did hang in the balance.

During my entire childhood, adolescence, and even adulthood, I had one basic problem. Or rather, I perceived it as a problem—I felt completely and fundamentally different from most of the people around me. I kept meeting with this fact all the time, and I didn't know how to deal with it for many years. It wasn't very long ago that I finally figured out beyond a shadow of doubt that that is what my life is actually about—being different.

I had the feeling that I didn't fit in anywhere. I had the feeling that nobody understood me. I had the feeling that I probably wouldn't be able to live here. I wasn't able to make compromises in any of my attitudes. I kept switching between all the possibilities and variants of two opposite poles: sometimes I felt completely incompetent, dumb, good-for-nothing, and unacceptable to the world around me, that is, for other people. Other times, everybody else seemed equally stupid, incompetent, and unacceptable. I was trying to find "objective" truth. I kept searching for what is "right." I was searching for how things "should be right."

I remember that when I was in fourth grade, one of our morning classes was canceled and the entire class agreed to take advantage of the time by going to our local park, which was near school. I lived in Prague 7, in Holešovice. It's the well-known Urania Park. On the way there, somebody came up with the idea of buying cigarettes or checking to see if any of our classmates had any with them. That time I separated from the class because I was sure I didn't want to go through that kind of an experience and I wasn't interested in trying anything like that at all. Back then, I simply knew it. So the kids went to the park, and I went home. Looking back at it now after all this time, I can still recall the look on my teacher's face when she was writing notes home to all the children's parents—except for mine—that they had gone smoking in the park during break. All the other children told her I wasn't there; she simply accepted this as a matter-of-course and without any comment. I took it as completely obvious too, as an expression of my freedom to choose; even my classmates didn't feel the need to react to me being different. My classmates never said anything bad about me, and I think I was very well liked. Back then, I was still aware of all that . . .

Today I know that I am the one who created all my problems. As time went on, I started having problems with being different. Instead of just letting other people worry about it, I began to think myself about how other people see me, and I thought that I must seem rather strange. For example, once during a school party, I didn't want to drink any alcohol simply because I didn't like the way it tasted. I felt these alternating attitudes in me: an unwillingness to accept the world around me and seeing the world around me as unwilling to accept me. I felt alternately superior and inferior to the world around me. I fell for the illusion, one most people accept, that I would only be able to come to an agreement with the others if I were to be exactly like them. But I didn't want to do that, so I was trapped—alone in this horrible world . . .

Now what? Once I realized that the things that other people did were unacceptable to me, I finally recovered from the feeling that I was strange, and I got settled with the feeling that others were strange. That's when my career of "fixing others" began, since I rarely come across anyone like myself. (Today I know that there isn't anybody else like me.) I thought that if I explained to them that getting drunk with table wine at parties, smoking in the park, visiting construction workers in their caravans—and a host of other activities I didn't agree with—were not the best things in the world to do, then they would change and I'd finally have the friends I'd always hoped for. As I already mentioned, I lived with my family in Holešovice. It was a relatively poor working-class neighborhood, and it's very possible that these children's interests were also affected by this fact. Today I understand that this tactic would never have worked; even so, the children usually respected me and some even felt "guilty" that they weren't as good as I was. And I started dreaming about having beautiful relationships, perfect partnerships, friendships, and I started composing my first poems . . . Some of my classmates and friends started calling me a dreamer, claiming that I didn't know anything about the facts of life, that I was naive and stuck in the past. Some of the tough girls, in particular, those who had made the rounds of the construction workers' trailers, took it as their responsibility to patiently explain to me that my view on relationships, love, and life in general was completely off. They kept pointing out, for my own good of course, how life really worked . . .

And you know, I almost believed them. I guess I'm a dreamer, and everything I want is crazy and just some pipe dream, because the real world looks completely different. But I didn't like it at all—so I committed myself first of all to my dreams.

I created my own world, where I'd escape to. Somewhere in the corner of my mind I still believed it could be real. I dreamed of fantastic relationships full of understanding, I dreamed of true friendship, I dreamed of the beauty and wonder of nature, I dreamed of finding a mutual understanding where words would be superfluous, I dreamed of happiness, I dreamed of men and women, I dreamed of love . . .

I was fascinated by the lives of other people, so I spent hours upon hours talking with them. Even when I was a little girl, I used to come home from school hours late because I had stopped to visit one or another of our grandmotherly neighbors. I knew all about their sicknesses, what they were going to cook for lunch, what was new with the kids. I became an expert on the web of their relationships. My mom couldn't help but be surprised by the number of grandmas in the neighborhood who would talk about me and tell her what we had been talking about. People were interested me, but at the same time, I kept distancing the world around me from my dream world. I couldn't manage to connect the two together. I saw so much pain, so many problems around me, and so much splendor and happiness in my romantic dreamworld.

I think my parents didn't have it easy with me. I remember how much I would read and read, and after coming home from school, I could easily just sit around for an hour, daydreaming; sometimes I'd have one pants leg on and the other one off, and I would be out "there," daydreaming again. That never failed to make my father mad. Whenever my parents would get angry with me and want to punish me somehow, they'd send me outside. I could sit at my desk for hours and hours, drawing my world. They had nicknamed me Princess Scribbler, and going outside for no reason in particular was a loss of valuable time for me, and I didn't like it at all. One of my girlfriends and I spent years drawing our own lands, during which we came up with everything you could possibly find in the land, including a government. We each had our own fashions, a magazine, navies (because our countries were islands), architecture, language, and so on. We stuck with the activity for a long time.

Finally, my father decided that I had to play a sport. He saw it as a way out of my spaced-out life. So I started my career in sports. I began playing volleyball. The beginning stages were hard; the fact was that I didn't want to play volleyball at all, so I made no effort whatsoever in order to prove to my father that it wasn't for me. But he wouldn't give up. He patiently stuck with me through the beginning, and because he played volleyball quite a lot, he wouldn't let any opportunity pass to hit the ball around with me and support me. I was totally uncoordinated, and my coach was desperate. I was lucky that he was interested in having tall girls on the team. So after a couple of years, I finally managed to get the basic techniques down, and results started coming in. On top of that, I started to enjoy playing. I learned how to concentrate, overcome fatigue, win, loose, believe in myself, pursue my goals—to want something and do something to get it. Sometimes we competed in rain and foul weather, at other times in sweltering heat. Our individual skills worked for the success of the team. I was proud of myself, the other girls, and of my father for making a decision and standing by it. I connected with myself, my body, and the world didn't seem as strange as it had before because I was standing with my feet firmly planted on the ground. I loved my volleyball world.

But my doubts returned. They returned when we girls started having more serious relationships with boys. Once again, I returned to my split world because I didn't like what I saw around me. I kept dreaming about my Prince Charming riding a white horse, and I only participated in real life when it was unavoidable. I didn't want to give up my dreams, and so I avoided more serious experiences. At the time, I didn't know anything about how people attract experiences based on their expectations. I didn't know that if I stop believing the right man could be out there, then he will simply stop existing. I wanted understanding, friendship, sincerity. I was taking things too seriously. I started feeling oddly different again. I couldn't understand how my girlfriends could have one- or two-day adventures that didn't lead to anything meaningful and make "random" acquaintances during tournaments and training camps, which ended as simply as they began . . . Back then, I just didn't get that each and every one of us is just different, and some people do things one way and other people another way. I didn't understand that I had the freedom to make my own choices, that I could independently decide which experiences I wanted to go through, and that I didn't have to search for "the right way of doing things." I didn't know that there is no right way of doing things and that I can decide based on my own likes and dislikes. Once in a while, some daring soul would presume to test to see if I really meant it. I would reaffirm that I really meant it.

Now what? The more I held fast to my illusion of a perfect relationship, the stranger I found myself to be. "I'm going to have to change something," I decided. "So then, let me give life a try," I said, and I shifted the borders of my inaccessibility. At that time—I was already twenty by then—a really nice guy appeared in my life. I think that he fulfilled my dreams. We lived in the same house together. It was a wonderful time in my life. He knew how to draw beautifully, and he would send me sweet letters with little drawings, hidden in different spots all around the house. We had long talks about everything imaginable, and we got along very well. I knew that he cared about me a lot, and he supported all my ideas. He was helpful, he had great parents, and being with him was wonderful. The problem was that the cancer that was my doubts had grown to such a stage that just as I started doubting my dream. I had started doubting the reality I had created. In other words, I started having doubts about my boyfriend. "Isn't it a little strange? How come he's so supportive of me? How come we get along so well? How come all the different things I do don't bother him?" He understood me most of the time. He was understanding all the time. And he understood back then too . . . We broke up. I knew it was idiotic. I knew that I was giving up on my dream. I knew that I would miss him, but I did it in spite of all that. I wanted to be normal. But we continued getting along well. We continued to respect each other. We remained friends. He remained my dream . . .

So I ventured into life. I let myself have one more relationship, where I was accepted and respected, but it wasn't as ideal as it had been during my first one. But I wasn't even able to maintain that one—after a year, we broke up. I think the thing that puzzled me the most in both relationships was that my partners accepted and supported me. In fact, I recall that I thought it was odd . . . I kept abandoning more and more my dream of beautiful relationships.

I had other relationships, all of which were gradually worse and worse. With each new relationship, my partners and I got along less and less; I accepted them less and less, and they accepted me less and less. At one point, I started having very superficial relationships and random encounters. I now know that they came into my life as leftovers from my volleyball career, when I scorned those types of relationships that my girlfriends had. Whenever we condemn something and think it's strange that somebody could possibly "manage to do something like that," then we actually attract similar experiences into our lives.

The goal of life is acceptance, accepting everything and everyone! Accepting doesn't mean being like someone else. We obviously have the opportunity to choose how we want to lead our lives. But at the same time, let others have that same choice without condemnation or judgment.

And then I met the man who would become my husband. There were few things we actually agreed upon. There were just a few ways in which we respected each other. On our first serious date, he even explained to me how much he'd like his girlfriend to be a small blonde, which I certainly was not. Despite that, we started dating. We attracted each other in a peculiar way—and today I know how powerful the mutual attraction of each of our life's lessons is. We sometimes have the feeling meetings are designed by fate, but I think everything consists of the strength of the lessons we ordered, which our partner is potentially able to provide us with. This was definitely a lesson. Our relationship was a battle for mutual acceptance. We both wanted love, understanding, and sympathy, but probably neither one of us believed we would get it. We either fought together or gave up parts of ourselves. Although I think I was the one who adapted the most, both of us probably did it to a degree. The only way to achieve peace, and my husband's love, was to accept his ways and ideas. We had made it clear that acceptance didn't mean becoming like him, but that's how I understood it back then. I continued to lose more and more of my power. I tried to adapt more and more, and I tried not to protest. True, I wasn't successful all the time because I continued to hope that one day my husband would change and understand who I truly was. I know that I didn't accept him even though I honestly tried to. I kept trying to figure out why he thought the way he did, and I kept pushing away my dreams of mutual understanding and respect.

We had three children together. I kept hoping that one day it would all change and we'd finally understand each other. But the situation seemed to be getting worse. My husband's business commitments meant that he was at home less and less. Our relationship began to function on a simply organizational manner, but I had become rather dependent on him after all those years and I couldn't imagine leaving. We become dependent on our partner when we give ourselves up in the relationship, when we adjust to such a great degree that we have the feeling that left to our own devices, we would get lost. Losing yourself in a relationship is like when employees lost interest in a business: they don't have any working morale, so then a dictatorial boss comes in and repressively pushes them back toward themselves. Likewise, in a relationship, your opposite partner helps you discover who you actually are. Most of the time, a partner wants the other one to submit and to keep accommodating more and more, and eventually that becomes intolerable. Then the suppressed partner finally stands up for who she/he truly is. Only when we are suppressed do we realize once again who we are not, and then, eventually, who we actually are.

I couldn't keep losing myself. I couldn't keep living without mutual understanding. And I couldn't live without my own dreams. I started to remember. I felt like someone else's property, and I had done this to myself. I had displaced myself from the relationship by not being myself. If I had remained myself, I probably wouldn't have been in that relationship. My husband found another woman, and I thought I wasn't going to be able to bear it. Everything had caved in, and I did not understand why it happened . . . After all I had done? After all that effort and self-denial? Precisely because of that! Precisely and only because of all that self-denial. Only later did I come to understand that if you give up yourself, that means that you don't respect yourself and therefore no one else can respect you either. I had deserved it. The most amazing thing had in fact happened to me so that I could understand what I was actually doing with my life. Thank you for that lesson. Consequently, I vindicated my work; I stood up on my own two feet. I vindicated my dream, and my children were smiling! **"I'm alive!"**

Now I'm living with a new partner again, who loves me for who I am, respects my ideas, and supports my chosen path. I am once again doing what I enjoy. But this time, I know that it isn't strange. It's normal—at least for me.

Today I know that I don't have to just dream my dream, but that I can actually live it, because what I do and create in my life is up to me . . . **I'm living my dream!**

Chapter 20

_&3 c&2_

Our Relationships

Relationship comes from the verb _to relate_. When you relate, it is with something; if there is a relationship, then the participants are mutually relating to each other. I often hear people say, "I just don't have a relationship with him . . ." This really isn't possible, because not having a relationship is a relationship too, in fact. And what's more, every relationship is a two-way street—which means that it works mutually, both ways. Often people explain their relationships, saying something like "I really loved him, but he wasn't interested in me at all," or something like that, as if she was unsatisfied, but he was fine with it. I think that if we are going to relate "truly" and in harmony with universal laws, it isn't possible for one person to be happy and the other not at all—because they are relating mutually. If it does happen, and we know that it does happen, it means that somewhere there is a disturbed balance and that one of the partners, or both, is making a serious mistake. The mistake isn't in the partner, however, but in the person themselves, in their relationship toward themselves, in their self-worth and self-love. How is it possible that she loves someone who doesn't love her? Why does this person call her attitude "love" and "to love," when she is being rejected by the other? Why does she have so little self-worth that she calls "to love" something that is actually just a masochistic attitude if she is being rejected? Relationships are a two-way street. To love means to give, but also to receive, and if one of the parties doesn't feel love, the other one can't feel it either. If they do, then that feeling doesn't have anything to do with love . . . So our relationships are a reflection of our relationship with ourselves, and this means that our relationships are functional or dysfunctional depending on our self-esteem, what opinions we have about ourselves, and how we understand ourselves. In our relationships, we get as much love as we are willing to give ourselves.

That's why it is futile to try and get an ideal relationship in our lives if we have confusion within ourselves. It is futile trying to make someone really love us if we don't believe we are worthy of love. It is futile to wait for love if we believe that we don't deserve it. Our relationships with other people are a reflection of our own relationship with ourselves. We can tell by the way others behave toward us what kind of opinion we have about ourselves. Through relationships, we come to know ourselves, our mechanisms. Often we find that people constantly attract similar partners or similar situations into their lives, things that they have already lived through repeat again and again. If the person doesn't learn from this and figure out what is causing the repetition of similar situations or people in their lives, then they build up the impression that that is simply how the world works . . . If we aren't willing to change anything in ourselves, our relationships can't be changed either. We are still sending out the same energy and therefore attracting the same kind of people who hear "our call." If, for example, you are a woman with low self-esteem, who comes from a family with six children, where you tried to earn your parents' love and equality with younger siblings by taking care of your younger brothers, then even in your relationships, you have the feeling that you have to earn the love of a man. It can happen then that you will attract into your life again and again men who will need support and rescuing. They will be unsuccessful and financially dependent, and you will take care of them. You will repeat this again and again until you figure out that you are actually a valuable woman who doesn't need to work for her love and that you don't need to save someone in order for them to love you. Start playing the game of admitting the truth to yourself, and every time when you find yourself excessively taking care of someone, ask yourself what you want to get in return. Because we would never have done anything extra if we didn't think that it will "pay off" for us.

If we have a negative experience from relationships in our childhood, which mostly relates to our parents' models, then, if we don't want to end up like they did, we can choose to go a different way, that is, to simply avoid relationships. It is important to point out that we all have some negative experiences, even if we don't consider them to be negative. Often it happens that our desire for love and acceptance, and because of this, also our ability to adapt, is so huge that we lose ourselves and we stop distinguishing what is good for us and what isn't. We even often begin to think that it is our fault that others can't give us love. And can you imagine how these people's relationships look . . . They are full of criticism and nonacceptance, without love and joy. They are full of disappointment and rejection. Disappointment is a reflection of our misplaced expectations, and rejection is a rejection of ourselves.

Sometimes we decide to reject relationships even before we go through "disappointment"—we are so certain knowing it will come that we don't even bother to get into it. And yet we don't feel good alone most of the time, as if something is missing. We stop developing because we don't get any information about ourselves. We fear the reactions of other people because we know that they are reacting to us. We want to have some influence on people around us and to change them, but we know that it can't work because we are only capable of changing ourselves. Of course, that is if we want to . . .

Once, a young man, a student of archeology, came into my consulting room. He really loved his chosen field and expected to have a good career ahead of him because he really enjoyed and was fulfilled by his studies. But he constantly felt tired and joyless. He had the feeling that something was missing, but he didn't know what. During the initial testing phase, we found out that he didn't have a relationship—he was missing a relationship with a girlfriend. He explained to me that he really didn't have a girlfriend, and he added obstinately that he didn't want one either. I was surprised a little, because I don't see this attitude very often. Most people are unhappy because they want someone and don't have anyone. But this young man didn't want anyone. Of course, I was interested to find out why! Initially he was stubbornly silent, but he understood the seriousness of the problem, and finally blurted out, "I don't know what I would do with some pea-brained girl who would keep me from doing what I like . . ." I looked at him, astonished, "Why would she be a pea-brained girl? Why would she keep you from doing things? And why would you even want a pea-brained girl who would keep you from doing things?" He looked at me, not understanding. "I don't want her, but she would do it," he replied. "And why do you think she would do that?" I asked again. "Because they all do that," he answered nervously. "And why don't you order into your life someone who wouldn't do something like that? Why don't you order someone who would support you and be glad that you have work that you love?" I urged him on. "Because that kind of woman doesn't exist, so it's better to be alone," he finished, quietly and resigned. And there it was . . . and I am not at all surprised that the young man didn't want to have a relationship. We create our reality ourselves, and in this case, even if a wonderful young lady were to come along, someone who would be willing to support someone they love in what they love to do and not to hold him back, this woman for sure wouldn't appear in this young man's life, because in his reality, no one like that exists. Imagine that this young man is ordering his love from the Universe and at the same time he is, through his subconscious programming, sending out the following requirement: "Send me a great girl, I want a girlfriend, but don't forget that she has to pester me about work, because I don't believe that it could be any different." The Universe understands and fulfills our every wish. You will get it. And the young man knows it, and that's why he would rather have no one. When he understood what he would have ordered, we worked together to change his order. You can probably guess where his attitude came from. His mother and father played this game together where the weak father wasn't able to assert himself with his interests, and mother, unfulfilled in her own life and activities, prevented the father from doing what he loved. But he probably didn't love his activities that much if he let himself play the game with her. The boy took the father's side and saw the mother as the enemy. Whenever we take sides with one of our parents, it's as if we have given up half of our brain. So, dear father, be yourself, and no one will stop you from doing things! Take care of your interests! Why do you feel guilty about liking your work? Your wife has the same opportunities as you do! Giving yourself up will make you both feel bad, and you won't solve anything for her that way. Grant yourself a support—but your own. No one will ever be able to support you if they are not fulfilled in their own lives. We can't love anyone more than we love ourselves, and if we think that we can, it won't work . . . The young man changed his program. "Now I know what I want, and I know I will find her, and that she definitely exists." Great, I am keeping my fingers crossed for you . . .

This story is but one of many where we almost consciously avoid relationships, because based on our experiences from childhood, we don't believe that our relationships could be purposeful and pleasant and that we could be accepted and loved.

The way in which we avoid relationships that we fear can sometimes be much more refined; it looks as if it's not our fault, because it is simply "impossible" to realize our goal. Once, a woman came to see me, complaining that she couldn't find a wonderful man to bring into her life. She was forty years old, and from the way she was telling her story, I had the feeling that her whole life she had done nothing other than to hunt for this great guy. She was so tired from this lifelong looking with zero results. It turned out the same way every time, because the one and only thing she was able to achieve was constantly meeting and having relationships with married men. It was her life problem, and she said it wasn't fun at all anymore. But at the same time, she explained to me that this state of affairs was perfectly normal because at her age there aren't any nonmarried men around. Just this statement alone would be enough so that other men would not appear in her life, because—as is the case in the previous story—in that case, in her reality, there can't be other kinds of men. Her stories were almost funny, because she kept meeting more and more men who, even though at the beginning they pretended they were single, later admitted that they were married. This fact was so stressful for this woman that she attracted these married men like a magnet.

We don't do anything we don't want to do. I asked her why she needed the married men in her life and why she constantly gave them so much energy. She got mad—but to be able to get to know something in our lives, we have to start asking questions. Those who don't ask questions don't get answers . . . Finally, she agreed that her "problem" must be benefiting her in some way, and we continued asking. Finally, we came to the big problems between her parents, which had really made her suffer as a child. Her house was full of arguments and tension, screaming and discomfort, fights between her parents. She didn't want a relationship like that. If we experience a very strong model in our childhood, even if it didn't suit us at all, most of the time, we just couldn't imagine that relationships can work another way. "Security is a machine gun," the lady said to herself, "and I would rather have nothing than have this." And there it is! So these married men actually worked rather well for her even though it didn't seem so at first . . . She can't come out on top in the end in a relationship with a man by attaining what she is most afraid of, that is, sharing her life together with a man.

A life together . . . We would have to search for a long time in order to find out everything people imagine under the concept a life together. There is no such thing as a 100 percent "correct" definition; there are just functional and nonfunctional definitions. Some people see a relationship with a partner as a limitation in their lives, and they assume that they will definitely lose the freedom they had before. Of course, you can guess what kind of partner people who think like this choose for their lives—because the Universe fulfills our every wish. Some people assume that now they have to conform to their partners in everything. Perhaps for them, this rule applies that relationship equals loss of yourself (if you want the relationship to work). Some people think a relationship is a compromise, and others, perhaps, that, "I have to dominate in order not to be dominated . . ." etc. What is it like for you?

Our conceptions, that is, our definitions of relationships and therefore our intentions too, which determine our choices and thus create our reality, are usually different in women and men. Many people are controlled by their so-called roles, which serve as a substitute for a real attitude of a man or a woman in a relationship. Most people have an image of what a "real man" or "real woman" should look like, or have an idea of the "right way" they should each behave. These roles make a free choice for them impossible and prevent them from being able to express themselves. And what's more, the people involved most of the time think that this is an "objective" fact, and they don't consider the possibility that other people could have different attitudes. Many relationships are controlled by "That's the way things are done, everyone does it like that . . . that's normal." Most people then don't even think about whether they actually want it like that too. Some women are consequently sentenced to a lifetime of standing at the stove, not having their own opinion about anything, and many men are sentenced to be despotic and require daily service from their wives, to be noncommutative and to read their newspapers, even if, as is often the case, they aren't interested in them, but most of the time, "everyone" does it that way. It is just normal. Our roles have an infinite number of variations, and they control even the relationships of people who "don't want to do it like that." They are then careful not to be like "everybody else," and they have to "insist on" their unusual counter-roles against others.

Stop playing roles! Become free in your relationships. Clarify, find, and name what is right for you, and stop pretending. Figure out what you both really want, and start doing it. Don't fight about whose idea is "right;" just agree about what you want it to be. Whatever you want. You are the only two who decide. Just the two of you create your relationship. Just you two have to agree; that's why you should cooperate and not fight. Be flexible and keep only those positions that serve you, and be only in the kind of relationship that you will be happy in.

Some people are convinced that a partnership has to be for life, and so they try to stay in relationships that haven't worked for them for a long time, and they suffer. A relationship is our mirror, and it is only through a relationship that we can come to know ourselves and to make use of our potentials. How often do we hear around ourselves, for example, "I can't do that, because Tony doesn't like it" or "He doesn't want me to" or something similar. We give up our own power and "do it because of them". Don't be afraid to move on. Don't be afraid to want more. Speak with your partner about your ideas, your plans, about what you want. It took a long time for me to overcome that system of belief that said that my relationship was for my entire life. It took me a while to understand that I can want more, that I don't have to conform if that is not good for me. We don't live for relationships that limit and torture us, where we feel unaccepted. I think that the goal of our lives isn't a partner relationship, but our personal growth and our path, in which our relationship can really help a lot. After you have freely asked for everything you need, after you have figured out what you want, and if you can't come to an agreement with your partner, it is time to move on. Get rid of your limitations, the reasons you can't get what you want, because we will get as much love in our relationships as we give ourselves

> **because pleasant, kind relationships full of love and understanding exist, but that's on the condition that you stay yourself and that you accept your partner as they are . . . and if it fits together, then that's it.**

Chapter 21

How to Get an Answer

Those who ask will get to know! Those who ask questions get answers!

The problem is, however, that many of us are not asking the questions, so those people are not getting answers—and what's more, in many cases, they don't actually want an answer at all. Maybe you know the feeling from your own life when you have an inkling that something is wrong, but you don't want either to ask about or consequently to get to know what the reality is, because you are scared that you'll find out something that would hurt you. Such a situation can come up in your relationship, for example, when you're suspicious that your partner is seeing someone else. The suspicion eats you up inside; it's ruining you, but in spite of that, you don't take any steps to find out the truth. In most cases, things will "fix up" somehow, and in the end, you will find out everything you need to know, whether you like it or not. By accident . . .

Every change that happens in our lives is a consequence of all our previous steps. What is currently "just happening" in our lives is always somehow connected to us even if at this very moment we don't know how. So you can say that

if we don't want to see what is happening in our lives right now, then in fact, we don't want to take responsibility for our past decisions and choices.

We don't want to connect our own lives with what is coming. We don't want to know which of our steps led us toward those specific results or, as the case may be, what we aren't going to repeat because it turned out badly and we didn't like it at all. We don't actually want to learn! Our life is just about causes and effects, and if we refuse to take responsibility for this fundamental causality, then we are in fact refusing life itself. We can't create what we want in our lives, because most of the time, we end up being victims, who are at the mercy of this "terrible" world. But even after that, some people won't give up and decide to fight against this "injustice." Their life becomes a hell because they are always on the lookout for those who have done them wrong, who could have hurt them, or been unjust, and so on. Consequently, they can't be themselves, and they can't focus on their own creation.

But let's go back to the beginning, that is, to our initial unwillingness to find out how things really are. What all in fact happens when we play dead out of fear of finding out something we don't want to know? Why do we refuse to participate in our own lives and let the outside world decide for us? Why don't we want to know the truth so that we can participate in our life through our decisions? When we do this, we give up our own power and become dependent on our surroundings. And then we are right to be afraid of pain, because if we let others decide, then we know for sure they will not decide according to what we want, but according to what they want. And that, of course, won't always be the best thing for us. In the example of a partner being unfaithful, if we take the position of the one who doesn't see or hear things, most of the time, we are actually collaborating on the whole thing and, in this way, enabling our partner to continue in the other relationship. It can also happen that our partner may think that that is actually okay because "we don't mind." If we don't react and we don't solve the issue out of fear of pain, then what follows is often even greater pain, because during the process, we lose the self-esteem we had left. We're actually not willing to learn from the resulting situation, because the very fact that our partner found another relationship outside of us means that we are actually not equal partners and that mostly we give our partner too much room. I don't mean merely the physical space, but mainly the feeling of our importance in the relationship. Most of the time we give our partner preference and back off from our demands until we have eventually displaced ourselves from the relationship and left enough space for someone else to step in. I often hear "I did so much for him, I didn't want anything for myself, I put up with everything, who else would do that for him?" Sometimes it is so hard to explain to these people that it is exactly for those reasons that it happened, because "If I feel unimportant, other people will behave towards me as if I am not important." And people stop needing the unimportant person...

And so, learn! Take responsibility and ask **why.** Ask in time, whenever something doesn't seem right to you. Don't be afraid to find out the truth about yourself and other people. You don't want to live in fear, do you? Because the biggest fear comes from your inability to solve things. Whenever you don't like something in your life, ask where you have made the mistake, where you have gone against yourself, because it is our own denial and lies that cause us to lose the most strength. We are the most tired when we do things with which we don't agree with on the inside and we don't know how to stop. Whenever you can't get out of some kind of situation, it means that you are repeating the same thing again and again ... so ask.

Ask! But who? Maybe you have already tried going around to all your friends, but you aren't satisfied. No one can tell you what you should do, because what is good for one person isn't necessarily good for someone else. Other people are a mirror for you, but they won't solve your problems. You have to decide for yourself. So the only person whom it makes sense to ask is yourself. If you are missing some information, go out into the world, but then ask yourself again—what do you think about it?

But how to ask? Only a small part of our decisions take place on the conscious level (it is reported to be 20 to 30 percent). The rest of what we know and what is controlling us takes place on the subconscious level. How often we affirm something that is what we think that we think, but our reality doesn't agree with it. How is that possible? We have to find the source of these discrepancies and put everything in order.

How do I do it? In order to find the source of my clients' complaints, I am accustomed to use a kinesiology test. In this way, we can define very precisely where the biggest problem is and which life attitudes are causing the current problems and complaints. Using the muscle test, we can bypass our belief systems that don't allow us to admit the truth. It is a natural phenomenon that our body is weakened by negative information and that strong muscle is our reaction to positive information. You know it from your own reactions when someone says something that is not nice to you, and you feel weak and incapable of movement. Often times people who are about to give you some really bad news ask you beforehand, "Are you sitting down? I need to tell you something." On the surface, you can behave as if it doesn't bother you, but your body betrays you. Weak muscle means simply that there is some kind of problem, and so we will keep searching. If we are clever in our questioning, we can get an answer to every question we ask. In our cellular memory, we remember every second of our lives, and we can play that recording again if we need to. The body reacts to every unambiguous question that relates to our past or present. Testing muscles can't take the place of our deciding about our future because we create the future only by what we will do. We do the muscle test in order to once again get in touch with the feeling that we have when we really are speaking what we feel. It is wonderful to see with other people, that magic **aha**, when we name the real problem or destructive mechanism in their lives, and they understand how it actually functions in their lives. We know this anyhow on the subconscious level, so as soon as we bring it all into consciousness, the whole issue doesn't seem strange to us at all. It is a wonderful feeling to become aware of the truth and to feel the possibility of changing what doesn't work. It is a wonderful feeling when we understand the imbalance that we are anyway feeling, because it has been making us feel uncomfortable. It is wonderful to return to your power through understanding. It is wonderful to be home again . . .

But we can't always change things simply by understanding them. Sometimes we have to look deep into the past when we lived through something that we couldn't overcome and the pain remained. Fear also remained, and our bad model, through which we try to avoid our fear. Sometimes these are very serious issues, such as the death of someone close to us, war, or very complicated relationships that caused us to give ourselves up. Therefore, we weren't able, in these difficult circumstances, to stay true to ourselves and to hold on to our pride. It is so hard for a baby to keep its pride when its parents have decided that it was born "at the wrong place and wrong time," and they put the child in an orphanage. This is a hard lesson for this child who has to learn that they are valuable and equal with everyone else, even in these circumstances, and that they shouldn't bring down the actions of their parents on themselves and on their own self-esteem. It is so hard . . . But I believe that all these problems can be solved. During my sessions, when we go back to the time when we experienced the greatest pain, we let the built-up emotion go, and we find the right solution—that is, one that ensures that we don't give ourselves up. We return our energy back to ourselves, because there isn't a problem that can't be solved. Our brain will always show us the perfect situation based on which we can understand everything . . . and change our attitude.

Sometimes it is very simple because we really want to make a change in our lives already. When we get rid of an emotional block and understand the connections, we can feel as if the world has changed. I remember one woman who was in her fifties and still hadn't had any relationships with men. She was very unhappy about this, and she knew that what she feared most was having a sexual experience. She had the feeling that all men were just interested in "one thing," and so she avoided relationships with them. During the unblocking session, we had to go deep into her past. We looked back into generations on her mother's side. It was several centuries back. Time is a redundant variable from the point of view of our brain because what we are thinking about, our brain perceives as reality, and in general, it doesn't care when something happened. She remembered a young girl who worked in the fields. As the sun beat down, she was reaping hay along with some other villagers. All of a sudden, a dust cloud appeared in the distance, and a group of riders came in on their horses . . . They were soldiers. The girl stopped working and watched them. This was at a time when human lives, perhaps, weren't so valuable, a time of war and pillaging . . . The story from her library doesn't turn out well. The soldiers came after her, caught her, and did terrible things to her. Cruelty, ridicule, rape, pain . . . they even burned the hay. A burnt smell stayed in the room where we had been working. The lady cried over the girl's powerlessness. But? Where there is pain, there is usually something wrong on our side as well . . . so let's check it a bit. The story is a symbol that we have to figure out because it contains our mismanaged principle. In this case, it was insufficient protection on the part of that girl because the other villagers didn't wait for anything and ran for cover. Don't you think that she brought this problem on herself, just a little bit? Soldiers are soldiers, and war is war. No matter what the situation, we must live in such a way that we take care of ourselves—as best as we can in the given situation. And there it is! We don't have to fear anything in our lives if we believe that we are capable of taking care of ourselves. Maybe you object, "Even against a bunch of soldiers?" Yes, even against a bunch of soldiers. Because if I am a woman and I look around, knowing that I live in the time that I do, and I see a column of soldiers coming, then I don't hesitate and I get out of there. If I want to live, I will avoid certain situations that do me a disservice because I respect myself enough. How much pain comes into the world simply because people don't have enough self-esteem, and so they are willing to go through the pain . . . The lovely woman inhaled deeply, her eyes smiling, her tears fast drying. When we understand, then we don't have to be afraid anymore. Most of the time then, we can do things that we simply weren't able to do before. She took another deep breath. "So I will do it. So many guys, so little time . . ." She doesn't have to fear men anymore or be afraid that they will hurt her, if she believes in herself, that she will recognize a dangerous situation as the case may be, and behave accordingly.

And now we can go on. We will release the energy that we have put into our fear and our restriction, and we can use this energy for our creation in the present.

Unblocking or diffusion is so far the most perfect way I have found how to get to the root of the problem. I consider the muscle test to be a perfect source of information because through it, we can reveal long-denied and latent fears and negative attitudes. The ancient Maya people used this method to get valuable information. But it is the same as with everything else: even this perfect aid serves us only as a transient help on our path to personal growth, because in a certain stage of denial, we need to come to know again our "feeling of truth." As we move on, we need to rely on ourselves. From time to time, some people get stuck at a specific stage of certainties, for instance, on the certainty of the muscle test, and they stop relying on their own feelings. No method in the world will substitute for our own decision making and our taking responsibility. That is why it is important to have our eyes and ears open and to notice everything around us and to connect everything with our own lives.

Along with our ability to ask questions must come our willingness to accept the answers that come to us. Believe that they can come from anywhere, because if you have really asked for them, then they will find you. So learn to receive all sources, because they are endless and sometimes very strange.

I remember one small incident that, even today, makes me shiver. This was several years ago, when I was interested in various connections between driving a car and our own lives, and I was teaching the seminar "I'm Driving," where people would work on their limitations and fears connected with driving a car. The theme and the symbolism of this theme fascinated me because it is so connected with our responsibility to drive our own lives.

I myself was driving a lot in those days, teaching classes around the country. These connections were coming together nicely, and I was pleased with my progress. I had the feeling that nothing could stop me, that everything was going great. At the time, I was driving my Renault 19, which came on my journeys with me. I had started thinking about buying another car because certain problems were coming up. One of the chronic problems that kept coming up was that my reverse gear kept breaking down. I didn't understand the context exactly, but apparently there was some kind of cable there that somehow always got pulled out, and then my reverse wouldn't reverse. The problem always came up at the most inconvenient times, when I really needed to back up, and it was really hard to back out of the given situation . . . I got angry but didn't understand anything. I took the car to be serviced again, but it always happened again. You might be thinking that I should have gone to another mechanic . . . But I kept giving it back to the same guy. One time, it happened again. But that time, "my" mechanic was too busy, and so I said to myself that I will get round it—I don't need reverse! I drove for about a week without it. Have you ever tried it? Especially in the center of Prague, it's a lot of fun. You have to know exactly where you are going, and you have to concentrate all the time on the fact that you can't back up. I started to realize that backing up is actually a normal and quite a necessary thing. I started to become aware that there are some situations that I can't allow myself to get into because I couldn't get out of them. In the end, I was excited; I had done it. I proved that I don't need reverse all that much. The next week, I went to the repair shop. While the guys were fixing my car, I stayed in the shop, colorfully relating my experiences, what a great job I did and how reverse isn't such a total necessity. All the guys laughed except for one . . . He was buried deep inside another car; you could barely see him, and all of a sudden, his head popped out. I knew that I had never seen him before even though I had been coming to this garage a lot lately. He took in a breath and said, "Don't you think, Ma'am, that sometimes in life we have to back up in order to move on again?" Bang! He lay down under the car again and didn't say a thing. I haven't seen him since then. He hasn't showed up in the garage again. Was he really there at all? That's what they call a "message from the Universe." They couldn't look down on that from upstairs anymore . . . I guess today I know how important reverse is. In the car, but also in life . . . And what about **you?**

Ask, and you will get an answer!

Chapter 22

_ᴄᴏ cᴏ_

What Works for Me?

"Life does, I think . . ." just like it works for each one of you. If we accept the universal laws into our life and stop fighting them, then we can create a world according to our own ideas. We all have that opportunity. We all have that power. We can all set functioning rules for our lives. And we can transform, cancel, or set new ones as the need arises.

In my opinion, the most important and valuable thing about life is **accepting the world around us**. Accepting ourselves, others— simply everything. My friends, accepting does not mean that you agree with everything and conform to something even if you don't like it. On the contrary, it is only acceptance that enables us to decide to depart freely from something that is inconvenient for us, because in most cases, we devote an immense amount of energy precisely into what is inconvenient for us. Because if we don't accept something, then we bring about precisely what we do not want—that is, that certain something will appear in our lives. Stop being offended by what you don't like. Just understand that other people do things differently. Don't devote energy to what you don't want because by doing so, you invite it into your life. In my opinion, for example, if all women saviors who take alcoholic men into their lives would accept such men as they are and, consequently, not try to save them, then alcoholic men would maybe stop existing. By accepting them as they are—that means them and their drinking—then they would figure out that they in fact do not want them in their lives because living with someone like that is usually not worth it. What these kinds of men would be left with would be alcoholic women, whom they wouldn't probably want anyway. If they didn't have anybody to take care of them and save them, I think they would simply quit drinking. **So don't think about others who do things differently as your enemies (nor as people deserving pity)** because all of us have the opportunity to choose how we want to live! Once again, that doesn't mean you need to silently suffer through what you don't like. That doesn't mean that when you're waiting in line to buy a melon and the person in front of you is smoking in your face, and because you're working on accepting things, that you decide not to say anything despite the fact that you're about to suffocate. That doesn't mean that you won't take care of yourself and not tell him what you think about what he's doing. Let me just remind you that **opinions and positions of all people are equally valid—so take care of yourself, but don't feel animosity toward others!** Don't try to find out whose opinion is the correct one or more correct, but find the opinion that is functional for you! **Express yourself!** Communicate your view of things without making a fool of others or feeling like a fool yourself. Some people put other people down in an accusatory manner for making them feel like that around them. Why don't you ask them why they feel that way? Why do they doubt themselves when they feel that way? You have the right to think something different, and so do they.

Listen to others!

Not long ago, my daughter and I were out horseback riding; we had taken a young girl and her little pony along with us. She was probably in the fourth grade, and she had grown up with her little horse. She rides wonderfully, so we didn't have to worry about her at all. Only once, when we galloped ahead a bit, did she lag behind, but she caught up soon enough. Her little horse may be just a simple stallion, but he has quite a personality even though he's been around awhile. He's about three times as old as his owner. The weather was beautiful, and we were all having a great time. At the edge of a particular meadow, the girl caught up to us. She had a problem; her nose was bleeding. We stopped. Since we had nothing with us, like cold water, to treat a bloody nose, I asked her, "Can you try and remember what you were thinking about when your nose started bleeding?" From my own practice, I know that when someone's having nosebleeds often, it means that the person feels like they are not getting enough love, more often that they are having the feeling that other people don't like them. Blood is our life energy, and by breathing through our nose, we nourish our entire body and communicate with the entire world. The problem is initiated by a specific situation. The little girl looked at me, and I could see she was thinking about something. She wasn't defending herself against anything; you could sense total acceptance of all the information she was receiving. After a little while, her nose stopped bleeding. We rode on. The rest of the trip went by without incident, and we parted ways at the stable. But I had the feeling that she was still preoccupied with something.

The next morning, we met for a ride again. "So I thought about what I was thinking about when my nose started bleeding" was the first thing she said to me. "And now I know. I was thinking about the view I have from my little horse, and I was curious about the view from your horses," she explained poetically. In other words, after interpreting her statement, we discovered that she was bothered by the fact that she was riding on a small horse and couldn't keep up with us. She sniffled a bit, but then we talked about how people should be happy with what they have, which doesn't mean they can't want more . . . The next day, I offered her a ride on my horse. She was ecstatic. The fields had just been harvested, so she and my daughter had a nice race. She won. She became the first rider to win on my horse. She was happy, and so were we.

She listened! She didn't fight! I can already hear some adults who would have responded to my question with a flood of explanations. "I've had nosebleeds since I can't remember when. My mother's nose used to bleed too . . ." Or that they weren't thinking about anything at the time, or something to that effect. Other people would tell me not to ask stupid questions and do something about it instead . . . But what? The little girl listened, so she learned. Maybe the next time it happens to her, she'll remember all by herself, and maybe then it won't ever happen to her again . . .

Another thing that comes to mind is the importance of **here and now**. The only moment for living is now. The power of the present moment is enormous. Most people live **the past**, which is a source of endless excuses and limitations. It takes the form of different fears and negative experiences from the past. As a result, we end up not being able to do what we want to do in the present. Don't forget to do a thorough housecleaning from time to time in order to get rid of things that don't serve you anymore. Do this both in your mind and in your material reality. Everything is a symbol; if your apartment or house is a warehouse for old and useless items, then believe me, your mind looks just the same.

There are also people who live solely in **the future**. They live solely through their plans and fantasies, putting off their life "for later." They're usually lacking any drive because they have enough time to manage everything. This is a great way to find out, someday in the future, that it's actually too late to do anything . . . **So don't put things off! Don't put off solving issues you're uncomfortable with!** This is how I see it: the longer you let dirt lie around, the more and more usually piles up. By putting off your problem, you frequently do get rid of it temporarily, but in time, it will get bigger. Don't let your problems get "all stinky and rotten" because if you stay in the stuffy room for a long time, your sense of smell will become blunt, and you will stop smelling it eventually. After a while, you'll blend in with your surroundings, and even more, you yourself will turn into it—the stink, that is. It's simple . . .

How often do we see, for example, people involved in a relationship that doesn't gratify them, in which they aren't happy, but in spite of all that, they remain? First, they do it "because of the kids." Then because the kids have grown up. Then because they have to find another job first. Then because they just found another job.

Then because they have a house together . . . and then there's no point to breaking up at all. "We'll live the relationship out somehow, we're used to each other, we'll tough it out . . ." We're not here on this planet to "tough it out."

> **The ability to tough things out, to endure, isn't what makes us strong. What makes us strong is how well we are able to live our lives! So learn to say NO to things that don't work for you.**
>
> **In order to know what doesn't work for you, learn to not suppress your feelings. Your feelings are your most valuable and only advisers. Process your responses to your environment, and you will see your path.**

Preserve your dignity and always choose what's best for you. Have faith, knowing that as long as you do what's best for you, it will also be what's best for others. Everything always falls into place. Don't try to discover what's good for others because they are the only ones who know that.

Oh! The amount of time in my life I spent wondering what everyone else could do for themselves and what it would be like if they took advantage of that and how great they'd feel if they only managed. That's time wasted because they are the only bosses of their own lives. **Get rid of your expectations!** You won't be disappointed afterward because disappointment is nothing more than your own attitude. We feel disappointed when reality differs from our expectations. Don't be afraid and move on! Believe in your dreams, but don't manipulate reality with your expectations. If what happens isn't for some reason **that** what you want, don't give up! Keep going! And keep going until you get what you want! It's fun! It's a game! It's life!

The moment when I felt the greatest relief was when I understood I never need to lie again. I don't have to be afraid that somebody will find something out because there's nothing to find

141

out. If I myself agree with what I'm doing, then I'll stand behind each and every one of my decisions, even the ones that weren't the greatest. It's not that big of a deal. Next time, I'll do it differently because we are always learning. Live truth! Live your own truth!

Live in truth!

You won't have to be afraid of anything because it will just be the truth. You'll be radiating an unequivocal energy. People around you will feel good because you'll be readable to them, and the right people will support you along your path because you know what you want. Don't be afraid that you won't be acceptable to everyone to the same extent. Take responsibility and let people have the right to have their own opinion of you. Don't be surprised, for example, that if you say that you don't like smoking and that you're going to fight for smoke-free public spaces, then you're not going to be liked by smokers. That's normal; you can surely understand and accept that. They have a right to their position. But you do too . . . Once you and others really express themselves, the end result will be the sum total of everyone's energy. And that's what it's all about! It'll be the best solution at the given moment for everybody involved, so

express yourself!

Be a real part of this beautiful world. Be proud of your own truth. Live your own truth because life is the sum total of all our human truths . . .

A lot more things still come to my mind, but one word occurred to me at the same time:

gradually

and all the great magic of that word.

Thank you for reading this far. I look forward to our next meeting.

About the Author

"Zdeňka Jordánová, is one of the most successful Czech writers in the field of personal growth and motivational literature." Czech journalist Lucie Kunešová (Dreamlife.cz) calls Zdeňka philosopher among Czech authors and writes, "Her books on the art of living are disappearing from shelves. Her seminars and workshops are crowded . . . She writes stories about people for people. She writes in the language of children, old men, she writes stories in such a way as she truly perceives. As we open any book by Zdeňka Jordánová, we always have to be willing to take full responsibility for our actions and our life. Her philosophy is integrated and gives meaning to our lives." Zdeňka's books are full of stories, connections, and coherences and are helping people to realize the universal principles and to see one's way in life. They are inviting the reader to live a meaningful and fulfilled life. These books are helping many people in overcoming their dysfunctional attitudes and are inspiring them to find their personal path. Their veracity attracts thousands of readers who want to live in a genuine and meaningful way.

The first book *Discover Your Goal* became a bestseller. Subsequently published books include *My Money, Connections, Your Child as a Chance for You, Driving through Life or A Journey Through Life in Our Own Car, Man or Woman?, Love, Brat, Journey through the Centuries, There's Still Time,* and books (not only) for children *Sirinek on His Travels* and *Dog Fairytale.*

Besides books, Zdeňka Jordánová published also cards for children "There was a world once upon a time," which she drew and arranged so that wisdom in beautiful rhymes simply explains patterns of our life. They are touching the basic principles allowing us to perceive the real and genuine meaning of our life. You can also find the Cards of Success that can be utilized in everyday life. Her creation is very manifold and currently addresses a large number of readers with its veracity. Her last work is "Year and Its Rhythm," a beautiful calendar drawn and written by Zdeňka after her return from her journey to the North, to Scotland. It relates the year rhythm to the rhythm of our creation and, with its pretty picturesque pictures, invites us to the harmony with nature, the order that facilitates our creation—if we will not go against it.

Discover Your Goal, Zdeňka's first book, is in some way an introduction to the whole general subject named life. Zdeňka started writing books based on many years of practice in her personal consulting room, where she witnessed many "miracles"—miracles of transformation of many people. "Everything has its solution," says Zdeňka, "of course, if we want to." This approach is also evidenced in her life. Zdeňka lives now on her ranch with her partner, Peter, and her three children. She loves stories, connections, and when things are simply making sense. Zdeňka, writer and personal growth teacher, says, "I knew that the world must be different than it looks like at the first glance as early as a small child . . . I couldn't find it for a long time. That genuine and beautiful world that I looked for is hidden. It is hidden in us! And we can discover it, each of us!"

She is fascinated with the simplicity of things, and according to the author, everything indicates that it is time to return to our true essence. It is time to start to really create the world that we wish to have. It is time to really make use of all the gifts of this world and the beauty of living on the Earth. Everybody can touch the stars and discover his/her beauty. It is time to open our feeling and respect the rules of things that we got as a gift! There is still time to understand that we are creating everything around us with our intentions! Zdeňka loves her horses, her friends, and her family—her great cosmic family. And also wind in the crowns of trees and grass stems. Just listen for a while . . . Do you hear it?